500 GEMSTONE JEWELS

500 GEMSTONE JEWELS

A SPARKLING COLLECTION OF DAZZLING DESIGNS

LARK
BOOKS

A Division of Sterling Publishing Co., Inc.
New York / London

SENIOR EDITOR
Marthe Le Van

EDITOR
Julie Hale

ART DIRECTOR
Matt Shay

COVER DESIGNER
Celia Naranjo

FRONT COVER

Tom Munsteiner
Necklace: Scissors, 2008

BACK COVER, FROM TOP

Karin Worden
Flower with Aqua Leaf, 2008

Loretta Fontaine
Bishop's Lane Series: Zinnia Necklace, 2004

James Kaya
Birth, 2008

Petra Class
Blue Yellow Stars, 2008

Todd A. Pownell
Mountain Trail Sunset, 2007

SPINE

Shay Lahover
Untitled, 2007

FRONT FLAP

Lilly Fitzgerald
Multi-Colored Sapphire Necklace, 2008

BACK FLAP

Isabelle Posillico
Directions Brooch/Pendant, 2008

PAGE 3

Erica Courtney
18K Gold and Diamond Goddess Rings, 2005

PAGE 5

Karl Fritsch
Die Tränen von Pandora, 2004

Library of Congress Cataloging-in-Publication Data

500 gemstone jewels : a sparkling collection of dazzling designs. -- 1st ed.
   p. cm.
  Includes index.
  ISBN 978-1-60059-341-3 (pb-pbk. with flaps : alk. paper)
  1. Artist-designed jewelry. 2. Precious stones. I. Title: Five hundred
gemstone jewels.
  NK7310.A15 2010
  739.27--dc22

                              2009030868

10 9 8 7 6 5 4 3 2 1

First Edition

Published by Lark Books, A Division of
Sterling Publishing Co., Inc.
387 Park Avenue South, New York, NY 10016

Text © 2010, Lark Books
Photography © 2010, Artist/Photographer

Distributed in Canada by Sterling Publishing,
c/o Canadian Manda Group, 165 Dufferin Street
Toronto, Ontario, Canada M6K 3H6

Distributed in the United Kingdom by GMC Distribution Services,
Castle Place, 166 High Street, Lewes, East Sussex, England BN7 1XU

Distributed in Australia by Capricorn Link (Australia) Pty Ltd.,
P.O. Box 704, Windsor, NSW 2756 Australia

If you have questions or comments about this book, please contact:
Lark Books
67 Broadway
Asheville, NC 28801
828-253-0467

Manufactured in China

ISBN-13: 978-1-60059-341-3

For information about custom editions, special sales, premium and
corporate purchases, please contact Sterling Special Sales Department
at 800-805-5489 or specialsales@sterlingpub.com.

Contents

Introduction

When I was asked to jury this book, I thought that the task would be simple—even fun. Gems inspire such deep attachment in the people whose lives they touch that I knew I'd be overseeing a collection of innovative and inspired designs. Over time, though, my buoyant attitude gave way to a tumble of questions, and I began to find the selection process daunting. When considering gemstones, there are so many factors to bear in mind besides beauty. Science, cost, rarity, and mechanics also come into play. Plus, new gems are being discovered all the time. Today there are more than ever before.

So I did some research, hoping to establish a few guidelines before jurying. Most of the definitions I came across for the word gem contained the phrase "beautiful mineral"—a clear reference to stones like the diamond, a gorgeous turn on carbon, and the ruby, the lushest iteration of corundum. But for each definition I encountered, I could think of stones that didn't fit in. What about gems that were simply rocks, like lapis lazuli? Or those "gems" that were just organic-based matter, such as amber or jet? And how about popular materials like coral or pearl, which weren't even land-based? Should they be considered gems?

To make matters more complicated, I noted that some gems were classed as precious, while others were considered semiprecious—a term I particularly dislike. After all, wasn't the rarest, most perfect alex-

Thomas Herman
Turquoise Oak Brooch | 2008

andrite much more valuable than an emerald that was cloudy and dingy? Surely such an emerald wasn't "worth" much. And considering how common amethyst was—it's mined all over the world—could it be considered precious at all? What about a two-dollar-a-carat quartz? Wasn't it too cheap to be called a gem? Also confounding were elements like river rock and concrete. These common and (pardon me!) dull materials are often given royal treatment by designers and used in their pieces. I wondered if the jewelry that resulted could be considered precious.

Just when does a mineral grow up to be a gem? And who has the right to say so?

Sure, there's a lot of science involved, including the color grade as indicated on a gemologist's chart, and the definitions established by the American Gem Trade Association. But don't the whims of fashion also influence a stone's status? Just a few years ago the idea of setting a raw, industrial-grade diamond cube in silver or gold and calling it diamond jewelry was thought of as too avant-garde for the fine jewelry industry. (Thank you, Todd Reed, for expanding our horizons!) And even more recently, heavily veined or plain flat diamond slices that are now quite fashionable and viewed as precious were tossed away during the traditional diamond-cutting process.

These and other issues swirled around in my mind as the curating date approached. I knew that I'd be choosing from a huge variety of materials, not all of them clearly gemlike. Would it hamper my critical faculties? Would I get stymied?

I suppose I needn't have worried.

What struck me the most as I reviewed the vast range of designs submitted for consideration was that I loved all of the pieces, because they represented the incredible variety of materials on offer by Mother Nature. As I evaluated the wide panorama of gemstones—from diamonds cut to the most scientific and exacting standards to beryls left in their raw crystal states—I felt a sense of wonder. How did tourmalines and sapphires get their scope of colors? How did a stone-cutter decide whether to carve a piece, facet it, or just leave it alone? How did jewelers arrive at settings that enhance stones so well?

Fortunately, my curiosity didn't get in the way of jurying—it just enhanced the sense of awe that I was feeling. The lure of gems, I realized, is a strong one. They're the rarest material a jeweler can work with, but—more than anything else—they're beautiful, and this fact proved to be the key for me. It provided me with the clarity I needed to curate responsibly and give every item its due.

This doesn't mean that I came to the task without some pre-existing standards. I admit to being biased toward jewelry that's wearable and creations that seem effortless. For these reasons, I focused first and foremost on design. I eliminated submissions with complicated settings that seemed off-balance, as well as pieces with a disharmonious choice of stones. I also passed on affected treatments that showed off technique rather than good composition.

Harmony, simplicity, and ease of design—these are the qualities that appeal to me, as you'll find when you flip through this volume. On these pages, you'll discover jewelry that will make you go "hm?" and jewelry that will make you go "ah." You'll also find that there seems to be no limit to the ideas that can be expressed through gemstones. Sometimes a gem is used to finish a design, and sometimes it is the design—as when a picture agate completes a scene, a drusy becomes a landscape, or an opal mimics the ocean.

A rainbow of stones is collected here, set in just about any kind of material—precious and non-precious—that you can think of, including gold, glass, platinum, palladium, iron, resin, and silver. This book is your opportunity to view the bounty of Mother Nature as it's been reshaped and transformed by some of the finest artists in the world, all of whom bring different perspectives and sensibilities to bear on the creative process. Without a doubt, jewelry can be stimulating as well as beautiful, and this volume is filled with pieces that are bound to raise aesthetic questions. But take my advice: forget about the artistic issues, and allow yourself to be swept away, as I was, by the beauty of gemstones.

Cindy Edelstein

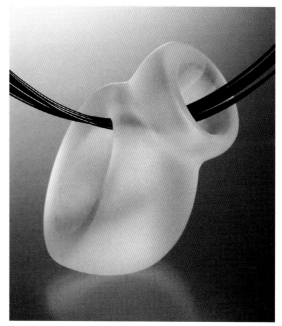

Dieter Lorenz
Carved Citrine Pendant | 2007

Sydney Lynch
Blue Bracelet | 2007

17.4 CM LONG

18-karat gold, 22-karat gold, sterling silver,
Paraiba quartz, aquamarine, peridot, keshi pearl,
blue tourmaline, rainbow moonstone, prehnite,
boulder opal, aquamarine surface; fabricated

PHOTO BY ALAN JACKSON

Ross Coppelman
Untitled | 2000
EACH, 4.1 X 1.6 CM
Boulder opal, Mississippi River
pearls, diamonds, crystal opals,
18-karat gold, 22-karat gold
PHOTO BY ARTIST

Suzy Landa

Petit Four Confection Bracelet | 2007

0.6 X 17.8 X 2.4 CM

18-karat gold, rubelite, pink tourmalines, diamonds

PHOTO BY BRENT KRAUSE

Julia Behrends
Overlap Rings | 2004
LEFT (PERIDOT RING), 3.3 X 2.4 X 1.5 CM; RIGHT (RHODOLITE RING), 3 X 2.2 X 1.3 CM
Peridot, rhodolite, diamonds, pink sapphires,
18-karat yellow gold; hand fabricated, laser welded
PHOTO ROBERT DIAMANTE

Suzy Landa

Stack of 25 Colored Gemstone Rings | 2008

LARGEST, 0.8 CM

18-karat gold, aquamarine, fancy sapphire, spinel, tourmaline, diamond accents

PHOTO BY TARA DIGIOVANNI

Laura Gibson

Rainbow Quail | 2004

43 CM LONG

22-karat gold, chalcedony, amethyst,
tourmaline, tanzanite, citrine, fire opal,
rhodolite, yellow beryl, chrysoberyl,
cat's eye, hessonite, mandarin garnet

PHOTO BY ARTIST

Emre Dilaver

Untitled | 2007

3.8 X 3 X 3.5 CM

24-karat gold, sterling silver, lemon topaz, diamonds; set, carved

PHOTOS BY LEVENT YÜCEL

Dara Dubinet

Citrine Abundance Ring | 2008

2.5 X 2 X 2.5 CM

Citrine, 18-karat gold, pavé diamonds;
lost wax cast, metalsmithed

PHOTO BY RICH WYSOCKEY

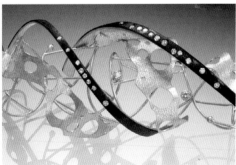

Jee Hye Kwon

Metropolis: Rhythm of People's Lives in City | 2006

4 X 54 X 3.5 CM

18-karat gold, shakudo, diamonds, sapphires; hand fabricated

PHOTOS BY RALPH GABRINER

Sarah Graham

Coral Rings | 2008

LEFT, 2.5 X 1.5 CM; RIGHT, 1.5 X 1.5 CM

18-karat yellow gold, steel,
diamonds; cast, fabricated

PHOTO BY HAP SAKWA

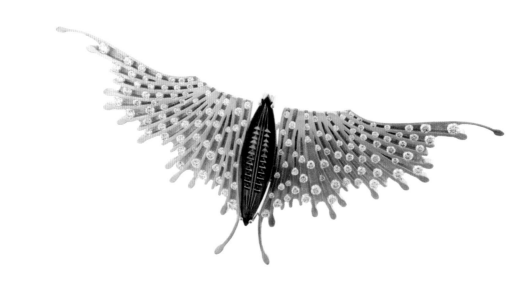

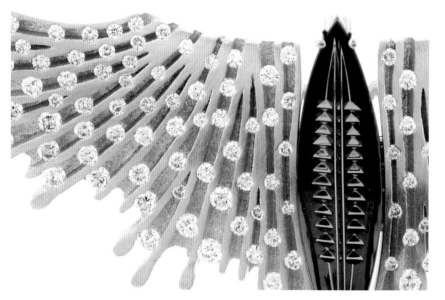

Christo Kiffer

Tourmaline Moth Brooch | 2007

8.5 X 3 X 0.9 CM

Green tourmaline, diamonds, 18-karat yellow gold; hand fabricated

PHOTOS BY ARTIST

**Peter Schmid,
Atelier Zobel**

Earrings | 2008

EACH, 3 X 2.5 X 1 CM

18-karat gold, platinum,
emeralds, diamonds; fused

PHOTO BY FRED THOMAS

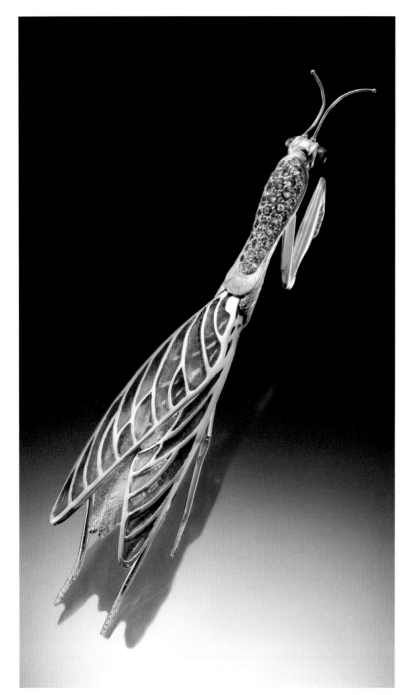

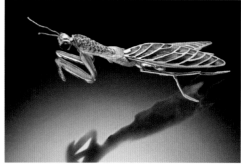

Leila Tai

Mantis | 2007

1.8 X 7.6 X 1.3 CM

18-karat green gold, gold tsavorites, blue sapphires, transparent enamels; plique-à-jour, hand fabricated, carved

PHOTOS BY RALPH GABRINER

James Binnion

Ring | 2007

2 X 2 X 2 CM

18-karat yellow gold, 14-karat palladium
white gold, sterling silver, platinum,
yellow diamond; mokume gane

PHOTO BY HAP SAKWA

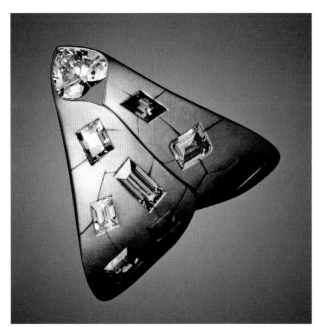

Pedro Boregaard

Camouflage Diamond Rhomboid Moth Pin | 1998

1.5 X 4 X 4.3 CM

18-karat gold, 22-karat yellow gold, sterling silver,
natural fancy-colored diamonds

PHOTO BY RALPH GABRINER

Katey Brunini

Object Organique Antler Ring | 2006

4 X 3 X 1.8 CM

Sterling silver, 18-karat yellow gold,
turquoise cabochon, rubies; bezel set

PHOTO BY PETER HURST

Thomas Herman

Beach Pea Brooch | 2008

6.4 X 4.4 X 0.8 CM

18-karat gold, boulder opals, blue chalcedony;
fabricated, chased, engraved, saw pierced

Barbara Heinrich

Lotus Leaf Earrings | 2008

EACH, 2.8 X 2.1 X 1 CM

18-karat yellow gold, diamond briolette drops,
diamonds; hand fabricated, chased, surface set

PHOTO BY TIM CALLAHAN

Lata K

Whimsy Transformable Flower | 2006

FLOWER, 2.5 X 1.9 CM; COLLAR,
38 CM LONG; BALL, 0.9 CM IN DIAMETER

18-karat yellow gold, diamonds

PHOTO BY STUART HEIR

Liaung Chung Yen

Flourishing #4 | 2007

3 X 2 X 2 CM

18-karat gold, diamonds, topaz;
fabricated, formed, forged, set

PHOTOS BY ARTIST

Liaung Chung Yen

Spring Journal #3 | 2008

5 X 5 X 1 CM

18-karat gold, aquamarine,
tourmaline, brown diamonds;
fabricated, formed, forged, set

PHOTO BY ARTIST

Hyewon Jang
Tower of Love Ring | 2006
5.1 X 2.5 X 1.3 CM
14-karat yellow gold, diamond;
fabricated, prong set, soldered
PHOTO BY PAUL AMBTMAN

Wendy Hung
Cinderella's Ring | 2007
3.9 X 3 X 0.7 CM
14-karat yellow gold, diamonds,
ruby, blue sapphire
PHOTO BY PAUL AMBTMAN

Petra Class

Big Blue Green Necklace | 2008

5.1 X 50.8 X 1.3 CM

22-karat gold, 18-karat gold, diamonds,
aquamarines, emeralds, tourmalines,
sapphires, pearls; fabricated

PHOTO BY HAP SAKWA

Joanna Gollberg

Greens Bracelet | 2008

7 X 17.8 X 2.5 CM

Sterling silver, semiprecious stones;
fabricated, oxidized

PHOTO BY STEWART O'SHIELDS

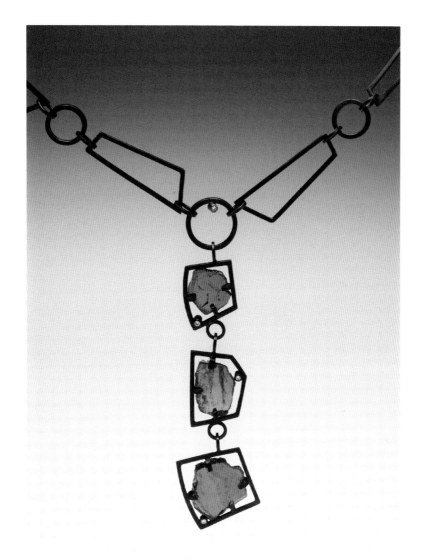

Daphne Krinos
Necklace | 2007
11 X 0.4 CM; 47 CM LONG
Silver, tourmalines, diamonds; oxidized
PHOTO BY JOËL DEGEN

Ming Lampson

Superman Ring | 2008

1.9 X 2 X 3.2 CM

Emerald crystal, 18-karat yellow
gold; carved, granulated

PHOTO BY ARTIST

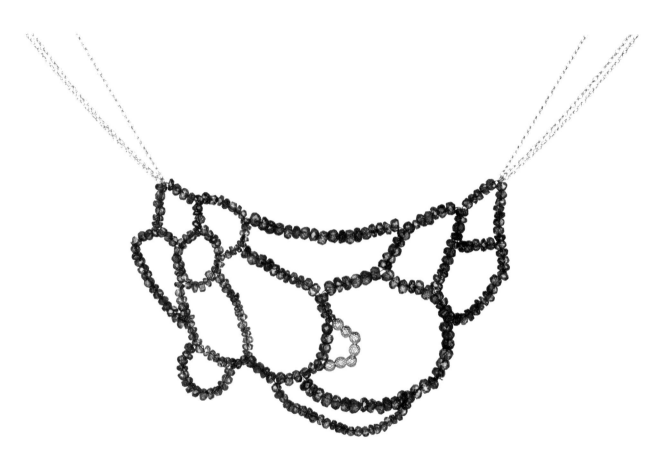

Melissa Borrell
Topography Pendant | 2007
7.5 X 4.5 CM
18-karat gold, 14-karat gold,
green garnet; beaded
PHOTO BY KENNON EVETT

Rian de Jong
From the Series NY-NY | 2008
4.5 X 3 X 1 CM
Cordierite, peridot, copper,
gold; electroformed
PHOTO BY ARTIST

Regine Schwarzer
Royal Jewel | 2008
32 X 32 X 1 CM
Chabazite, basalt, cubic
zirconia, sterling silver; cut
PHOTOS BY STEVE WILSON

Andrea Williams
Sa Stone Necklace | 2007

8.9 X 49 5 X 0.8 CM

Beach stones, sterling
silver; drilled, fabricated

PHOTOS BY MARK CRAIG

Pavel Herynek
Brooch | 1986
5.3 X 5.8 X 0.7 CM
Lepidolite, silver,
Grenadilla wood, steel
PHOTO BY MARKÉTA ONDRUSKOVÁ

Mary Hallam Pearse

Diamonds on Diamonds #2 | 2008

2.5 X 2.5 X 2.5 CM

Silver, aluminum, diamond,
14-karat gold, antique watch crystal

PHOTO BY ARTIST

Eva Tesarik

Time of Pearls—Necklace with Pendant | 2006

5 X 3.5 X 2.5 CM

Silver, pearls, rock crystal, photograph; sawed, mounted

PHOTOS BY BARBARA KROBATH

Claire Townsend

Encircle Me | 2007

2.5 X 2.5 X 0.5 CM

18-karat rose gold, 18-karat
yellow gold, star ruby

PHOTO BY MIKE GRAY

Yael Sonia

Natural Encounters | 2004

16 X 2.6 X 1.5 CM

18-karat yellow gold, quartz,
aquamarine, tourmaline, lemon
quartz; hand constructed

PHOTO BY ALMIR PASTORE

Erik Stewart
Hollein | 2008
3.5 X 4.3 X 0.8 CM
Palladium, colored diamonds
PHOTO BY ARTIST

Peter Schmid, Atelier Zobel

Ring | 2005

2.2 X 2 X 3 CM

Platinum, aquamarine, rough
diamonds; forge welded

PHOTO BY FRED THOMAS

Lisa Krikawa
Reine de Glace Locket | 2006
PENDANT, 6.7 X 2.4 X 1.2 CM
Platinum, 14-karat red gold, 24-karat yellow gold, 14-karat palladium white gold, blue zircon, blue sapphires, diamonds, Nyala rubies, ruby rondelles, Paraiba tourmaline; mokume gane, pavé set, bezel set

ZIRCON CUT BY JOHN DYE
PHOTOS BY HAP SAKWA

Michael Boyd

Untitled | 2008

2 X 2 X 0.6 CM

18-karat yellow gold, 18-karat white gold,
natural Montana sapphire; fabricated

PHOTO BY STEVE BIGLEY

James Kaya

Mirage | 2007

2.5 X 1.9 CM

Pink tourmaline, diamonds, 18-karat
white gold; hand fabricated

PHOTO BY ROBERT DIAMANTE

Annie Fensterstock

Stella | 2008

6 X 4.6 X 0.5 CM

18-karat yellow gold, 22-karat yellow gold, 22-karat white gold, diamonds, rubies, sapphires

PHOTO BY STEVEN P. HARRIS

Pamela Froman

*Harlequin Sunset Bracelet
with Harlequin Flare Ring* | 2004

BRACELET, 19 X 1 CM; RING, 2.6 X 2.2 X 1.2 CM

18-karat white gold, 22-karat
gold, orange sapphires, orange
citrine cabochon; crushed finish

PHOTO BY JAY LAWRENCE GOLDMAN, JLG PHOTO

Da Capo Goldsmiths

Embrace No. 1 | 2005

3.1 X 2.1 X 1.4 CM

18-karat yellow gold, citrine, rubies

PHOTO BY ARTIST

Samuel A. Shaw

How to Drag a Boat Through a Forest | 2004

19 X 15.5 X 1 CM

18-karat gold, pearl, geode, spinel, aquamarine

PHOTO BY ROBERT DIAMANTE

Katey Brunini
Love Affair of the Four Elements | 2006
EACH, 2.9 X 3 X 2.5 CM
Sterling silver, 18-karat yellow gold, 18-karat
white gold, South Sea pearl, yellow diamonds,
wood replacement opal, blue diamonds, seed
pearls, belemite and Paraiba tourmaline,
bi-colored tourmaline, rubies; bezel set

PHOTO BY VISKO HATFIELD

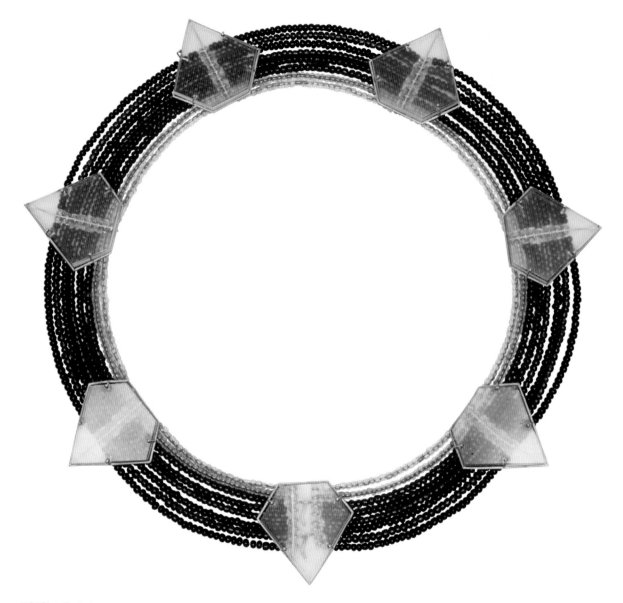

Philip Sajet
Rainbow Necklace | 1993
19 CM IN DIAMETER
Gold, rock crystal, beads; cut
PHOTO BY JAN OTSEN

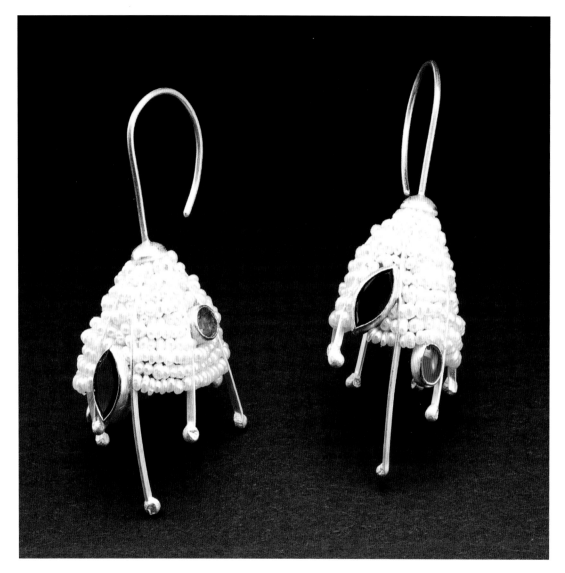

Boline Strand

Cupolae Earrings | 2008

EACH, 6 X 2.5 X 2.5 CM

Faceted rubies, tanzanite, garnets, carnelian
cabochons, 22-karat gold, 18-karat gold,
sterling silver; fabricated, beaded, bezel set

PHOTO BY TOM MILLS

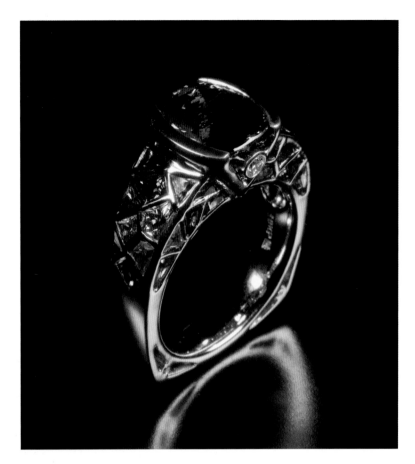

Philip Zahm Designs

The Stained Glass Ring | 2005

2.8 X 2.3 CM

Platinum, blue sapphire,
rainbow sapphire, diamonds

PHOTO BY MARK R. DAVIS

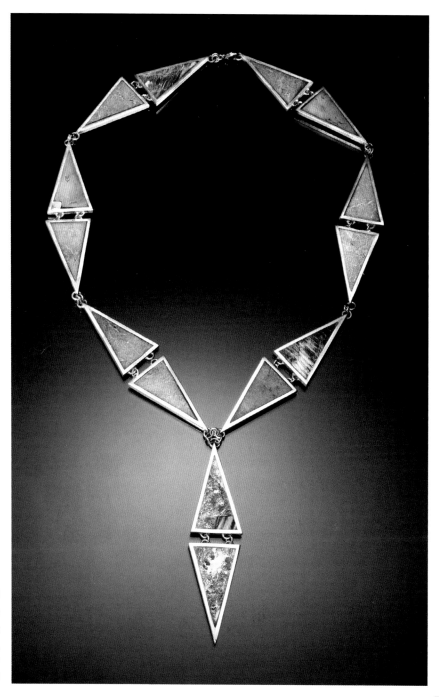

Kendra Roberts
Lavender Triangle Necklace | 2008
17.8 CM IN DIAMETER; 50.8 CM LONG
Lavender jade, turquoise,
oyster shell, sterling silver
PHOTO BY RALPH GABRINER

Regine Schwarzer
Brooches | 2008
AVERAGE, 4 X 3.5 X 1.4 CM
Fossilized coral, aventurine,
quartz, pink tourmaline, chabazite,
basalt, chrysoprase; cut
PHOTO BY GRANT HANCOCK

Janis Kerman
Earrings | 2007
EACH, 4.4 X 2.5 CM
18-karat gold, opal, aventurine,
tourmaline, industrial diamonds;
hand fabricated, assembled
PHOTO BY DALE GOULD, VISUAL ASPECTS

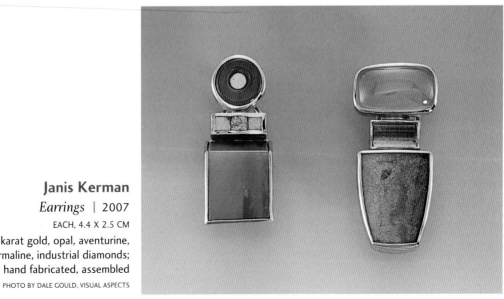

Michael Boyd
Untitled | 2007

4 X 3 X 1.5 CM

18-karat gold, 22-karat gold, sterling silver, Mexican opal,
black jade, mookaite, imperial jadite pebble; fabricated

PHOTO BY STEVE BIGLEY

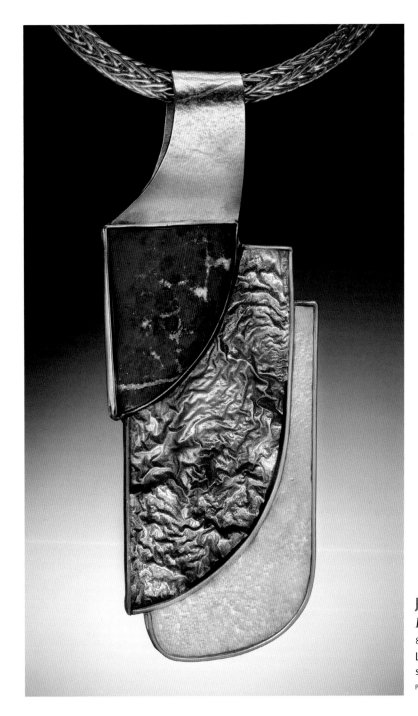

Judy Staby Hoch
Lapis Quatro | 2008

8.6 X 3.3 X 1 CM

Lapis lazuli, 18-karat gold, sterling
silver; hollow formed, fabricated

PHOTO BY RALPH GABRINER

Suzan Rezac

Necklace | 1998

0.4 X 48 X 2.7 CM

Lapis lazuli, 18-karat yellow gold,
sterling silver; oxidized, constructed

PHOTO BY TOM VAN EYNDE

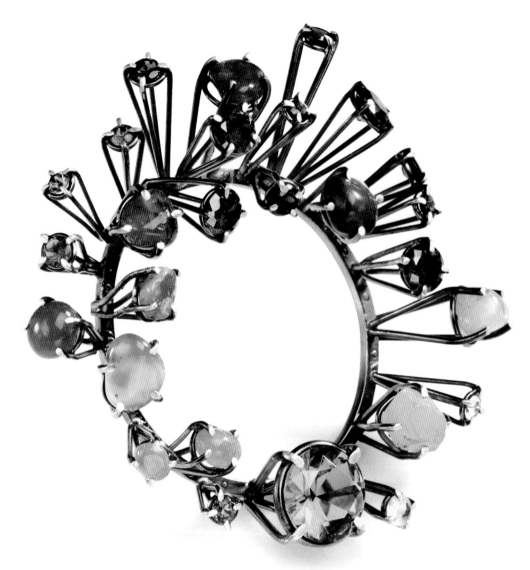

Joanna Gollberg

Reds to Yellow Brooch | 2008

7.6 X 7.6 X 3.2 CM

Sterling silver, semiprecious
stones; fabricated, oxidized, faceted

PHOTO BY STEWART O'SHIELDS

Suzan Rezac

Necklace | 2007

0.5 X 48 X 5.5 CM

Sterling silver, coral, gold leaf;
oxidized, constructed, pierced

PHOTO BY TOM VAN EYNDE

59

Karen Bizer
Cornucopia | 2008
EACH, 1.8 X 1 CM
18-karat rose gold, brown diamonds,
diamond filial; cast, pavé set, bezel set
PHOTO BY D. JAMES DEE

Min Kyung Kim
Untitled | 2008
1.2 X 2.5 X 1.1 CM
18-karat gold, keshi pearl,
diamonds; textured
PHOTO BY MARCO KANG

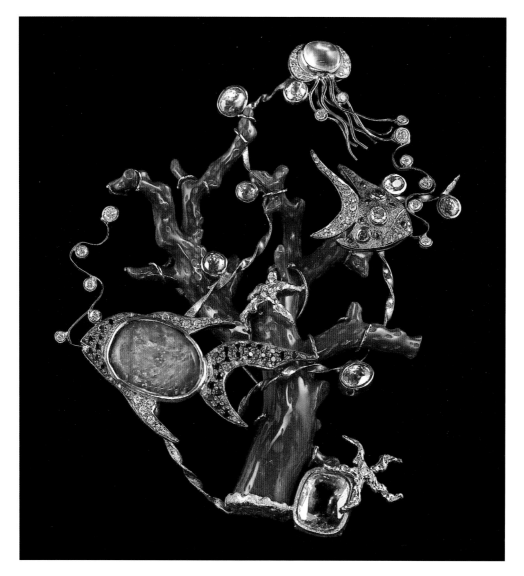

Cesar Lim

Negril en Tremblant Coral Pin | 2008

14 X 10 X 4 CM

Mediterranean coral, Australian opal, apatite, zircons, diamonds, moonstone, silver, 14-karat gold; hand forged, fabricated, oxidized, textured

PHOTO BY VLAD LAVROVSKY

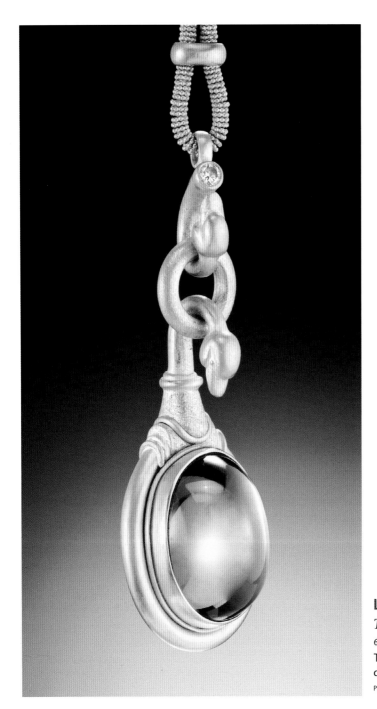

Lilly Fitzgerald
Tanzanite Swan Pendant | 2008
6.5 X 3.5 X 1.5 CM
Tanzanite, 22-karat gold,
diamond; hand fabricated, cast
PHOTO BY HAP SAKWA

Linda Kindler Priest

Golden Pond Brooch | 2002

9.2 X 3.7 X 1.5 CM

14-karat gold, natural yellow topaz
crystal, pale yellow diamond; repoussé

PHOTO BY GORDON BERNSTEIN

Pedro Boregaard

Galactica Moth Pin | 2000

1.4 X 8 X 3.3 CM

18-karat pink gold, sterling silver,
14-karat white gold, peach tourmaline,
blue sapphires, rubies, amethysts

PHOTO BY RALPH GABRINER

Jennifer Rabe Morin
Tourmaline Moth | 2008
5.7 X 6.8 X 0.5 CM
18-karat yellow gold, 18-karat white
gold, spinels, diamonds, watermelon
tourmaline; fabricated, inlaid, pavé set
PHOTO BY GREGORY MORIN

Anna Ruth Henriques
Song of Love | 2008
5.5 X 5 X 1.2 CM
18-karat gold, rock crystal,
mother-of-pearl, white
diamond, original painting
PHOTO BY GAETANO SALVADORE

Sarah Graham

Jacaranda Pendant | 2008

5.5 X 3 CM

18-karat yellow gold, steel,
diamonds; cast, fabricated

PHOTO BY HAP SAKWA

Sarah Graham

Jacaranda Hoop Earrings | 2008

EACH, 4 X 2.5 CM

18-karat yellow gold, steel,
diamonds; cast, fabricated

PHOTO BY HAP SAKWA

Julez Bryant
Dish Rings | 2007
Black diamonds, rose-cut diamonds,
fancy cognac diamonds, 14-karat gold

PHOTO BY ANDREA ROTENBERG

Ralph Bakker
Untitled | 2008
20 CM IN DIAMETER
Gold, tantalum, lemon quartz
PHOTO BY ARTIST

Pat Flynn
Trifold Cuff | 2008
3.7 X 6.3 X 5.7 CM
Iron, 22-karat gold, 18-karat gold, platinum,
diamonds; forged, fused, fabricated
PHOTO BY HAP SAKWA

Cesar Lim

Amoeba Ring | 2007

4.5 X 3 X 4 CM

Fine silver, 18-karat gold, white diamonds,
fancy diamonds, irradiated blue diamonds;
hand fabricated, textured, oxidized

PHOTO BY VLAD LAVROVSKY

Denise Betesh

Cluster Ring | 2008

2.5 X 2.5 X 2.5 CM

22-karat gold, labradorite rainbow
moonstone; granulated

PHOTO BY WENDY MCEAHERN

**Andréia Sutter
Roberto Sutter**

Canary Island Lava Bangle | 2007

9 X 10 X 4 CM

Lava from the El Teide volcano, diamonds,
18-karat yellow gold; cut, polished

PHOTO BY ROBERTO SUTTER

Josephine Bergsøe
Sea Creature | 2007

2 X 2.8 CM

22-karat gold, green
aquamarine, diamonds

PHOTO BY KRISTIAN GRANQUIST

Josephine Bergsøe
Conk Fish | 2007

1.8 X 2 CM

18-karat white gold,
22-karat gold, diamonds, ruby

PHOTO BY KRISTIAN GRANQUIST

Judith Kaufman
Yin-Yang | 2008
5.7 X 5.7 X 0.6 CM
Abalone shell, 18-karat yellow
and green gold, 22-karat yellow
and green gold, diamonds
PHOTO BY HAP SAKWA

Felicity Peters

Castellani | 2007

4 X 4 X 0.9 CM

18-karat gold, tourmaline; granulated

PHOTO BY VICTOR FRANCE

Alison B. Antelman
Triple-Pod Tourmaline | 2008
40 CM LONG
Sterling silver, 18-karat gold, 22-karat gold,
tourmaline; hand fabricated, oxidized
PHOTO BY ERIC SMITH

Petra Class

Diamond Mosaic Earrings | 2000

EACH, 3 X 2.5 X 1 CM

18-karat gold, 22-karat gold,
diamonds; hollow fabricated

PHOTO BY HAP SAKWA

Marianne Hunter

The Universe Dances | 2008

5.4 X 27.3 X 1 CM

Enamel, quartz with pyrite, diamonds, pallasite, rutile, fossil coral, hessonite garnet, 24-karat gold, 14-karat gold, 18-karat gold; fabricated, engraved

PHOTO BY HAP SAKWA

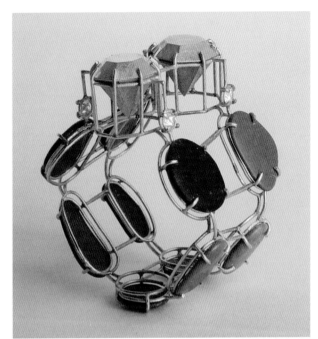

Philip Sajet
Silverstone | 2002

1.6 X 3 X 2 CM

Silver stones, pebbles, diamonds

PHOTO BY BEATE KLOCKMANN

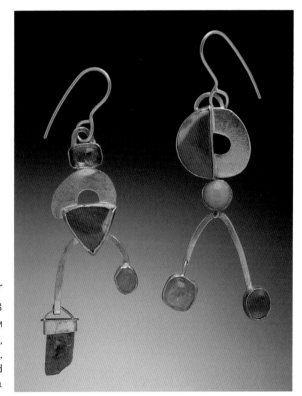

Carolyn Bensinger
Earrings | 2008

EACH, 5.5 X 3 X 0.5 CM

18-karat gold, 22-karat gold, mookite,
sapphires, tourmaline, ambronite,
imperial topaz; hand fabricated

PHOTO BY DEAN POWELL

Tiffany Peay
Untitled | 2007
48.9 CM LONG
14-karat yellow gold, tourmaline, smoky
quartz, chrysoberyl, garnet, citrine
PHOTO BY ARTIST

Todd Reed

Fancy Rose-Cut Earrings | 2008

EACH, 7.3 X 1.2 X 0.7 CM

Rose-cut diamonds, raw diamond cubes,
rose-cut rubies, 18-karat yellow gold,
silver, patina; hand forged, fabricated

PHOTO BY ARTIST

Jeannette Fossas

Asymmetric Earrings | 2005

EACH, 6 X 1 X 1 CM

Diamonds, platinum, 18-karat
yellow gold; pavé set

PHOTO BY JOCHI MELERO

Hema Malani

Swing | 2006

EACH EARRING, 4.1 X 1 X 1.5 CM; PENDANT, 7 X 1.2 X 0.4 CM

White diamonds, colorless diamonds, black diamonds, spessartite garnet, 18-karat white gold, 18-karat yellow gold, rhodium plating; bezel set, bead set

PHOTO BY ARTIST

Vicente Agor

Vesuvius Ring | 2007

3.8 X 2.5 X 1.6 CM

18-karat gold, blue diamonds, cognac diamonds,
Mexican fire opal; lost wax cast, hand carved

PHOTO BY MIKE PFEFFER

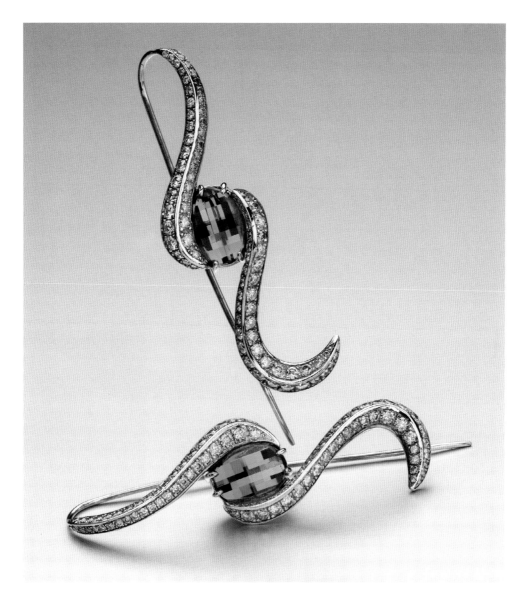

Mark Schneider

Tourmaline Switchback Earrings | 2007

EACH, 3.5 X 1.1 X 7 CM

18-karat white gold, white diamonds,
yellow diamonds, green tourmalines

PHOTO BY JOHN PARRISH

Marc Stiglitz

Away We Go Engagement Ring | 2008

2.7 X 2.2. X 1.7 CM

Platinum, ideal-cut round diamonds, black diamond;
hand carved, lost wax cast, bezel set, pavé set

PHOTOS BY GEORGE POST PHOTOGRAPHY

Da Capo Goldsmiths

Embrace No. 3 | 2007

7.5 X 3 X 3 CM

18-karat white and yellow gold, fire opal,
white diamond, champagne diamonds

PHOTO BY ARTIST

Gurhan

Periwinkle Y-Necklace | 2008

45.7 X 8.7 X 1.6 CM

24-karat gold, rose-cut white diamond,
brilliant-cut white diamond, peridot;
hand crafted, hand hammered

PHOTO BY ARTIST

Cathy Carmendy

Glamorous Scroll Rings | 2006

EACH, 1.8 X 1.7 CM

20-karat yellow gold, diamonds, lime citrine,
green beryl; cast, hand assembled, hand detailed

PHOTO BY ZALE RICHARD RUBINS

Kim Eric Lilot

Hokusai Tribute Necklace | 2008

45 CM LONG

18-karat royal yellow and white gold, rosé pearls, diamonds; pavé set, lost wax cast, fabricated

PHOTOS BY HAP SAKWA

Josephine Bergsøe
Galaxy | 2006
38 CM IN DIAMETER
18-karat gold, 22-karat gold, diamonds
PHOTO BY SARA LINDBAEK

Tamara Kronis

Crocheted Art Nouveau Neckpiece | 2008

PENDANT, 6 X 5 CM; NECKLACE, 41 CM LONG

18-karat yellow gold, chalcedony, moonstone,
amethyst, citrine, peridot, onyx, sapphire, ruby,
freshwater pearl, carnelian, garnet; crocheted

PHOTO BY PAUL AMBTMAN

Gitta Pielcke
Ring Valentin | 2005
3.8 X 2.5 X 1.9 CM
18-karat yellow gold, diamond-cut brilliants
PHOTO BY ATELIER PIELCKE-ZIMMERMANN

Devta Doolan
Three-Stone Black Diamond Ring | 2007
2.6 X 3.1 X 0.9 CM
22-karat gold, 18-karat gold,
black diamonds; cast
PHOTO BY HAP SAKWA

Christa Lühtje
Ring | 2008
2.2 X 1.4 X 2.2 CM
Gold, onyx
PHOTO BY EVA JÜNGER

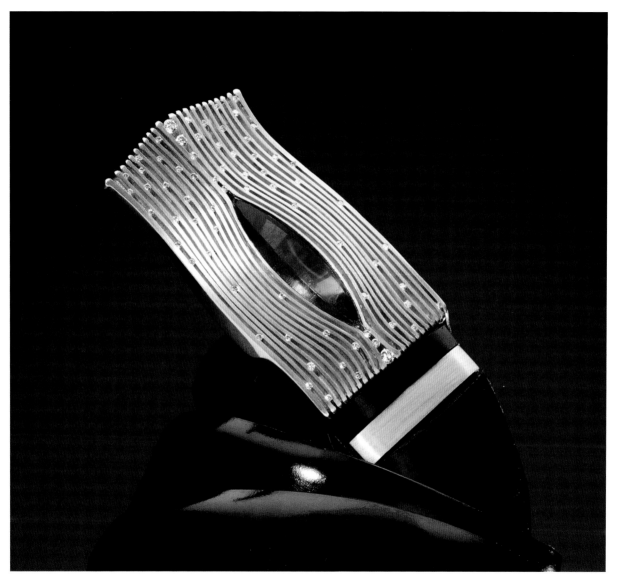

Christo Kiffer

Belt Buckle Spectrum Winner | 2003

6.4 X 3.8 X 1.2 CM

Gray tourmaline, diamonds, 18-karat
yellow gold; hand fabricated

PHOTO BY JOHN PARRISH

Jee Hye Kwon

Cocoon | 2006

EACH, 11 X 2.5 X 2.5 CM

18-karat gold, shakudo, shibuishi, diamonds; hand fabricated

PHOTO BY RALPH GABRINER

Claudia Steiner

2schwebende | 2008

2.7 X 3 X 3.5 CM

Tourmaline quartz, sterling silver

PHOTO BY STEFAN LIEWEHR

Cesar Lim

Two Pairs of Ribbon Earrings | 2007

EACH, 3.5 X 2.3 X 2.8 CM

Fine silver, 18-karat gold, diamonds;
hand fabricated, textured, oxidized

PHOTO BY VLAD LAVROVSKY

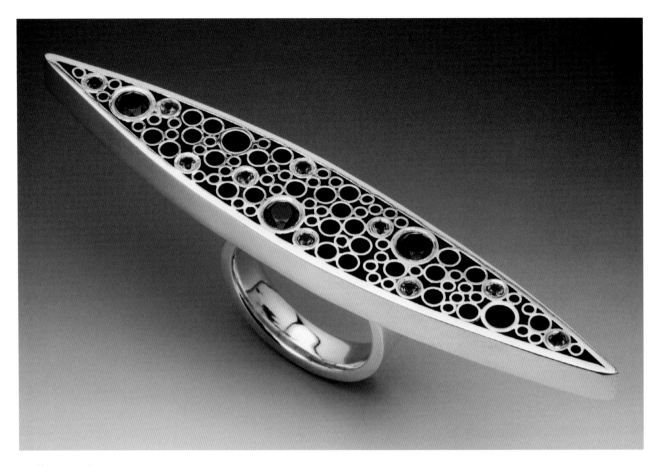

Belle Brooke Barer

Canoe Ring | 2007

2.5 X 6 X 1 CM

Sterling silver, garnet, citrine;
oxidized, hand fabricated, set

PHOTO BY GEORGE POST

Heather Guidero

Tangle Necklace | 2008

45 CM LONG

Sterling silver, ruby; hand fabricated, oxidized

PHOTO BY MARTY DOYLE

Susan Wise
Jeff Wise

Kalahari Aurora | 2002

8 X 4 X 1 CM

Black jade, red coral, diamonds,
18-karat gold; carved, sculpted, inlaid

PHOTO BY ARTISTS

**Susan Wise
Jeff Wise**

Prometheus Rose | 1998

8 X 4.5 X 1 CM

18-karat gold, black jade, red coral, lapis
lazuli, opal; carved, hand fabricated

PHOTO BY ARTISTS

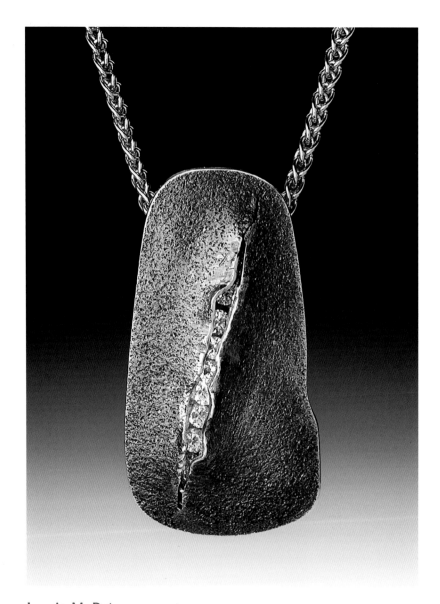

Laurie M. Peters

Below the Surface | 2007

4.5 X 2.5 X 0.5 CM

Sterling silver, 18-karat gold, 24-karat gold, diamonds; textured, oxidized, kum boo

PHOTO BY JOHN GOODMAN

Andy Cooperman

Lens | 2004

WIDTH, 6.25 CM

Bronze, sterling silver, opal,
diamond, 18-karat gold

PHOTO BY DOUG YAPLE

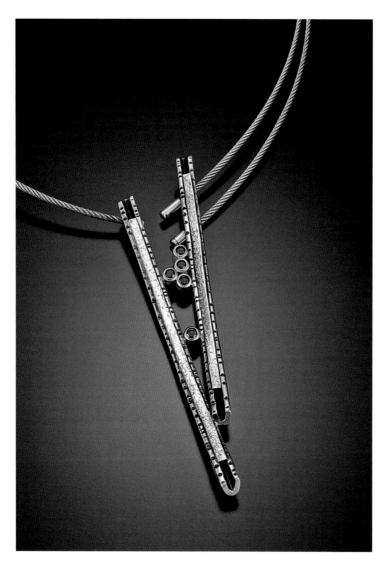

Davide Bigazzi

V. Necklace | 2008

PENDANT, 7.7 X 1.2 X 0.4 CM

Sterling silver, 18-karat gold, black
diamonds, steel cable; hand fabricated

PHOTO BY HAP SAKWA

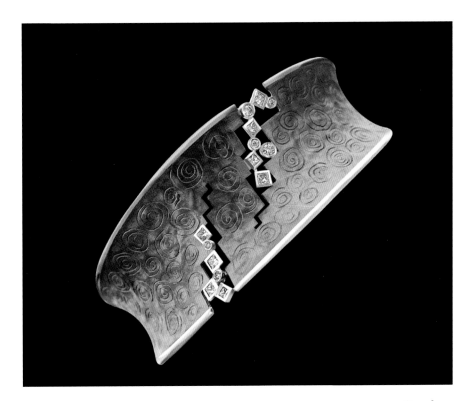

Cresber

To Sara Bracelet | 2007

2.5 X 6.5 X 5.5 CM

18-karat black gold, princess- and brilliant-cut
diamonds; hand fabricated, textured

PHOTO BY ARTIST

this attached gem will work with fold rings

Yael Herman

Swinging Diamond—Ring | 2007

3.5 X 3.5 X 2 CM

24-karat gold, diamond, stainless steel; laser pierced

PHOTO BY ARTIST

Tanja Emmert

Cinderella and Snow White | 2007

EACH, 2.8 X 2.8 X 1 CM
Cinderella: onyx, rock crystal, 24-karat gold
Snow White: rock crystal, 18-karat gold; hand cut

PHOTO BY JÜRGEN CULLMANN

Tanja Emmert

The Star Talers | 2008

2.8 X 2.8 X 1 CM

Rock crystal, diamonds; hand cut

PHOTO BY ARTIST

Vinograd Yasmin
Ring | 2005
4 X 3.5 X 1.2 CM
18-karat gold, plutonic stone
PHOTO BY MEIDAD SOCHOVOLSKY

Sara Borgegård
Brooch | 2008
6 X 5.5 X 5 CM
Wood, lime chrysoprase
PHOTO BY ARTIST

Vikki Kassioras
Deepest | 2008
PENDANT, 2 X 1.5 CM
18-karat yellow gold, sterling silver, obsidian;
fused, oxidized, hand carved

CARVED BY S. KOLIOPOULOU
PHOTO BY TERENCE BOGUE

Bettina Speckner

Brooch | 2003

2.5 X 4.5 X 2.5 CM

Pyrite, sapphire, gold

PHOTO BY ARTIST

Zuzana Rudavska

Crystal Pendant I | 2007

10.5 X 5.5 X 0.3 CM

Sterling silver, gold-filled wire, citrine,
labradorite, fluorite, aquamarine,
indigolite; interwoven, soldered

PHOTO BY MILAN MATASOVSKY

Marta Sanchez Oms

Blau | 2008

4.5 X 3.5 X 3 CM

Silver, cavansite, stilbite; textured

PHOTO BY ARTIST

Iris Bodemer

Untitled | 2008

26 X 24 X 2 CM

Sapphire crystals, cotton

PHOTO BY JULIAN KIRSCHLER

Eily O'Connell
Jailhouse Rock | 2008
4.5 X 2.5 X 2 CM
Silver, rough-cut aquamarine; cast, oxidized
PHOTO BY NORTON ASSOCIATES

Walter Chen
Untitled | 2007
3.5 CM IN DIAMETER
Silk cocoon, gold, diamond; dyed, set
PHOTOS BY ARTIST

Anika Verbrügge

Frida & Poldi Brooch I | 2008

3.1 X 6.4 X 6.6 CM

Silver, patina, copper, calcite;
bent, soldered, welded, mounted

PHOTOS BY FREDERICK HÜTTEMANN

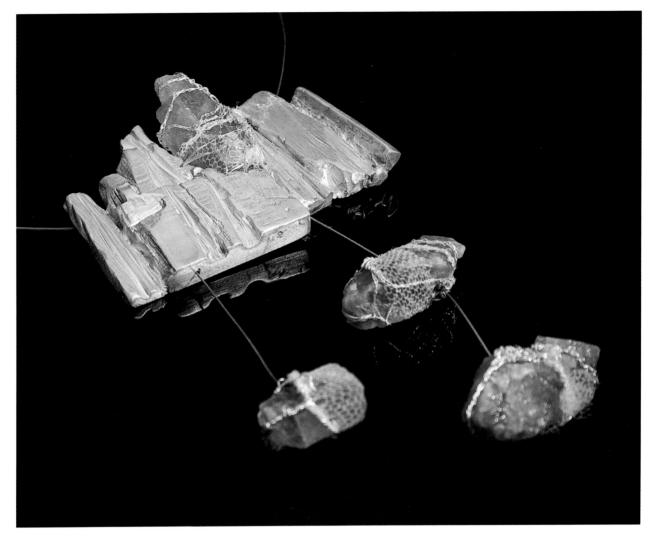

Mabel Pena

Glacier Detachment | 2008

14 X 7.5 X 1.2 CM

Sterling silver, fine silver wire,
aquamarine, tulle, steel wire; cast

PHOTO BY DAMIAN WASSER

Iris Bodemer
Untitled | 2008
29 X 22 X 3 CM
Aquamarine, shell, linen, copper
PHOTO BY JULIAN KIRSCHLER

Kathleen Rearick
Gnaw Series: Gut Ring | 2008
3 X 5 X 5 CM
Sterling silver, steel, gut, citrine; fabricated
PHOTOS BY ARTIST

Ezra Satok-Wolman

Afloat | 2008

3 X 2.2 X 1 CM

18-karat red gold, palladium, rough
diamond; mokume gane, forged, tension set

PHOTO BY ARTIST

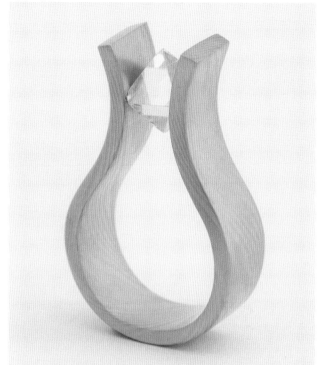

Karl Fritsch

Horschtigeckel | 2007

3.6 X 2.1 X 1.2 CM

Silver, rubies, patina

PHOTO BY ARTIST

Jennifer Kellogg
Silver Cage Rings | 2002
EACH, 3.1 X 2.1 X 1.2 CM
Sterling silver, yellow
sapphires, orange sapphires
PHOTO BY LUIS ERNESTO SANTANA

Anna Lorich
Nostalgia Brooch | 2006
7.6 X 5.1 CM
Sterling silver, felt, thread,
cushion-cut citrine; hand fabricated
PHOTO BY ARTIST

Beate Eismann

Letter (Brooch) | 2008

12.2 X 16.5 X 0.4 CM

Handmade paper, 8-karat gold,
aragonite, flourite, quartz

PHOTO BY HILTRUD UND JÜRGEN CULLMANN

Rian de Jong
From the Series NY-NY | 2008
6.5 X 6.5 X 0.5 CM
Peridot, copper, gold; electroformed
PHOTO BY ARTIST

Alona Katzir
Untitled | 2006
3.7 X 2.3 X 0.5 CM
Fine silver, rose-cut diamonds; Ashanti cast
PHOTO BY BOAZ NOBELMAN

Jan Matthesius
My Innerself (Hand Piece) | 2002
6 X 3 X 3 CM
18-karat gold, blue topaz, fire opal
PHOTO BY ROB GLASTRA

Stephanie Jendis
Necklace | 2005
43 CM LONG
Coral, tiger's eye, synthetic
stones, 18-karat gold
PHOTO BY ARTIST

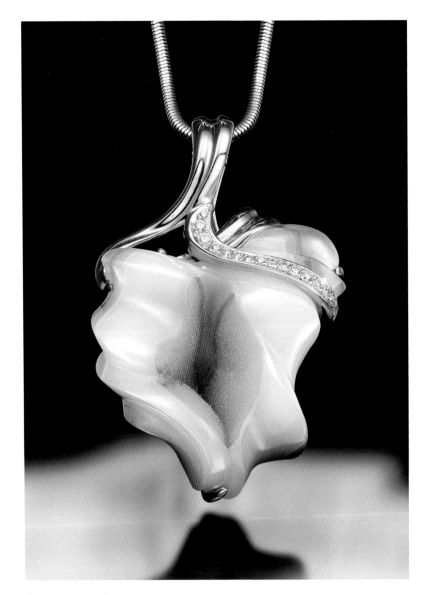

Samara Christian
Daffodil | 2007

3 X 2.6 X 0.8 CM

Agate drusy, 14-karat yellow gold, white
diamonds; lost wax cast, pavé set, carved

PHOTO BY CHRIS ADYNIEC

Christine Hafermalz-Wheeler
Agate and Opal Necklace | 2008
5.5 X 6.5 X 0.5 CM
Agate, Mexican opal, 18-karat gold; shibori
AGATE CARVED BY DIETER LORENZ
PHOTOS BY DAVID WHEELER

125

I love the orange and purple together

Barbara Heinrich

Fire Opal Necklace | 2003

43.2 X 1.9 X 1.9 CM

18-karat yellow gold, diamonds, fire
opals, amethyst; handmade, faceted

PHOTO BY TIM CALLAHAN

Lori Auster

The Moonflower | 2008

0.6 X 9 CM

18-karat gold, garnet; cast, carved

PHOTO BY RALPH GABRINER

Lydia Gerbig-Fast

Autumn Freeze Neckpiece | 2008

3 X 19 X 19 CM

14-karat gold, 18-karat gold bimetal, sterling
silver, enamel, copper, moldavite, epidote in
quartz; etched, torch fired, fabricated, bezel set

PHOTO BY ARTIST

Claire Moens
Haiku | 2008
11 X 4 CM
18-karat yellow gold,
dendrite agate
PHOTO BY ARTIST

Liz Bucheit

Autumnal Tiara | 2005

15.2 X 10.1 X 9.5 CM

Sterling silver, drusy quartz, pearls; forged, fabricated

PHOTOS BY PAUL NAJLIS

Marilynn Nicholson

Blooming | 2006

10 X 7.5 X 0.5 CM

Sterling silver, Coyamito agates, white
drusy quartz, 24-karat gold

PHOTO BY ANDREW NEIGHBOR

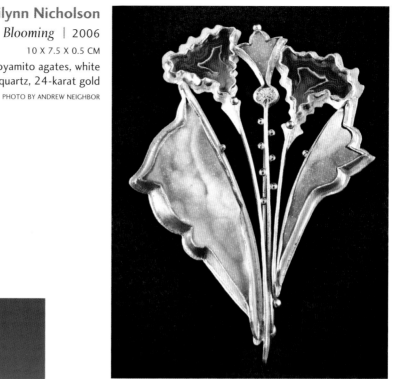

John Petet

Untitled | 2008

5.7 X 4 X 0.7 CM

18-karat yellow gold, agate,
tourmaline; carved, bezel set

AGATE CARVED BY DIETER LORENZ
PHOTO BY ARTIST

Samara Christian

Emmy | 2005

PENDANT, 5 X 2.5 X 0.7 CM

18-karat yellow gold, yellow diamonds, white diamonds, boulder opal, golden South Sea pearl; lost wax cast, hand carved, hand finished

PHOTO BY CHRIS ADYNIEC

Valerie Jo Coulson
The Gauntlet Cuff | 2003
6.5 X 7 X 0.8 CM
22-karat gold, 14-karat gold, Australian opals, black jade, chrysoprase, ruby, garnet; fabricated, inlaid, bezel set
PHOTOS BY CURTIS HALDY

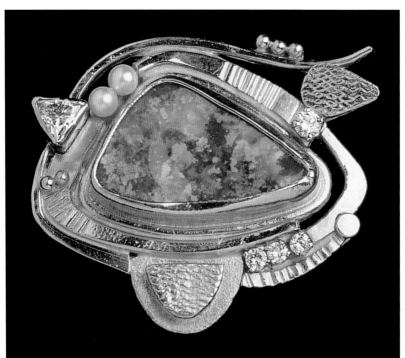

Ross Coppelman

Untitled | 2002

3 X 4.5 CM

Boulder opal, diamonds, pearls,
18-karat gold, 22-karat gold;
forged, fused, soldered

Pavé Fine Jewelry

Untitled | 2006

3 X 1.4 X 0.9 CM

14-karat white gold, 14-karat yellow
gold, natural green sapphire, white
diamonds; lost wax cast

Helen Blythe-Hart
Through the Looking Glass Neckpiece | 2004
MEDALLION, 7 X 8 X 0.9 CM; OVERALL LENGTH, 43.2 CM
18-karat gold, 22-karat gold, boulder opal, tanzanite, peridot,
tsavorite garnets, amethysts, sapphires, rhodolite garnets, diamond,
Tahitian pearl, natural pink freshwater pearls; hand fabricated

PHOTO BY ARTIST

George Sawyer

Untitled | 2002

20 X 25 X 2 CM

Aquamarine, 18-karat yellow gold, 14-karat
gray gold, Erotik beryls, Spirit Sun aquamarines,
platinum; mokume gane, hand fabricated

PHOTO BY ARTIST

Elizabeth Gualtieri, Zaffiro Jewelry

Empress III | 2007

11 X 5 X 1.2 CM

Blue moonstone, aquamarine, blue zircon, purple
sapphires, diamonds, 22-karat yellow gold,
18-karat yellow gold; fused, repoussé, granulated

PHOTO BY DANIEL VAN ROSSEN

I like the unusual shapes + settings

Patricia Tschetter

Something Old, Something New II | 2005

7 X 2.7 X 0.9 CM

Cobalto calcite drusy, iridescent pyrite drusy,
Idaho River rock, sugilite, tourmaline, champagne
diamonds; fabricated, granulated, domed, chiseled

PHOTO BY ROBERT DIAMANTE

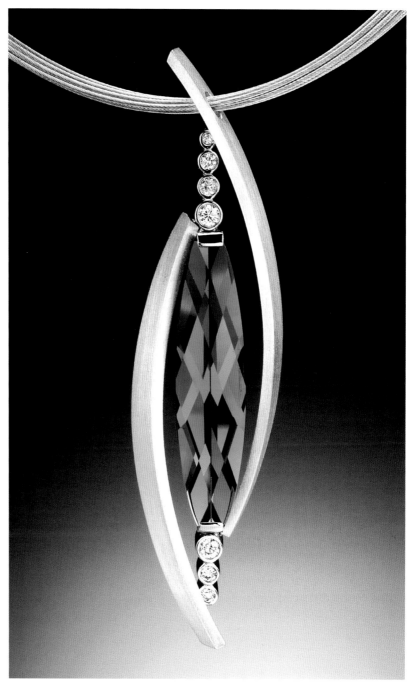

Adam Neeley
Tango | 2007
7 X 1.9 X 1.3 CM
Tourmaline, diamonds, Iris gold,
14-karat white gold; hand fabricated
PHOTO BY HAP SAKWA

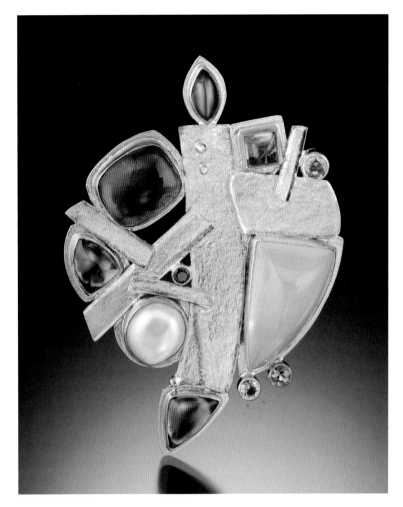

Isabelle Posillico

Directions Brooch/Pendant | 2008

5.6 X 4.5 X 1.5 CM

18-karat gold, 22-karat gold, green tourmalines, peridots, pink sapphire, aquamarine, pink tourmaline, pearl, ruby, rubelite; fabricated

PHOTO BY HAP SAKWA

Pamela Farland

Untitled | 2008

EACH, 7.5 X 2.5 X 0.4 CM

22-karat gold, tourmalines;
hand fabricated, bezel set

PHOTO BY KARIN WILLIS

Joanna Peters

Untitled | 2008

3.4 X 2.3 X 1.6 CM

18-karat gold, 24-karat gold, pink
tourmaline; carved, lost wax cast,
soldered, fabricated, claw set

PHOTO BY MYRTO APOSTOLIDOU

Phill Mason

Diurnal Temple and Nocturnal Altar | 1997

EACH, 4 X 2 X 2 CM

Diurnal Temple: Square step-cut citrines,
18-karat rose and yellow gold; hand fabricated
Nocturnal Altar: Round step-cut amethysts,
18-karat rose and yellow gold; hand fabricated

PHOTO BY ARTIST

Stephanie Albertson
Stack Rings | 2008
EACH, 0.6 TO 1 CM
22-karat gold, diamonds, colored
gemstones; handcrafted
PHOTO BY DAVID LEWIS TAYLOR

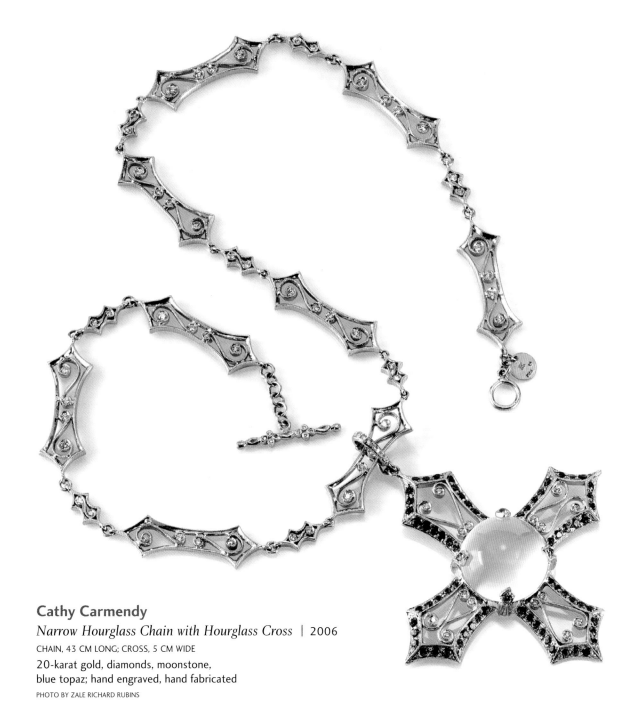

Cathy Carmendy

Narrow Hourglass Chain with Hourglass Cross | 2006

CHAIN, 43 CM LONG; CROSS, 5 CM WIDE

20-karat gold, diamonds, moonstone,
blue topaz; hand engraved, hand fabricated

PHOTO BY ZALE RICHARD RUBINS

Julie Rauschenberger
Octahedron Splitz Ring | 2006
2.1 X 2.1 CM
Diamonds, 22-karat gold;
granulated, carved, cast
PHOTO BY DOUG YAPLE

Pamela Froman
Venus' Cross | 2005
PENDANT, 7.5 X 3.5 CM
18-karat yellow gold, pink tourmaline,
pink South Sea pearls; crushed finish
PHOTO BY JAY LAWRENCE GOLDMAN, JLG PHOTO

Niyati Haft
Egypt | 2008
2.6 X 2.1 X 1.7 CM
18-karat gold, smoky quartz;
wax carved, cast, set
PHOTO BY KASHI-DIGITAL DESIGN

Jack Gualtieri, Zaffiro Jewelry

Fantasia Pendant | 2007

5 X 2.5 X 1 CM

Pink topaz, padparadscha sapphires, lilac garnets, diamonds, 22-karat yellow gold, 18-karat yellow gold; set, fused, granulated

PHOTO BY DANIEL VAN ROSSEN

Sharon Choisser
Treasure Bud | 2006
4.2 X 2 X 2.2 CM

Rose, yellow, green, and white gold, 24-karat gold, rubies, pink sapphires, shakudo alloy, copper, diamonds; mokume gane, cast, pavé set, fabricated

PHOTOS BY SUTTER PHOTOGRAPHERS

Mark Nuell
Untitled | 2008
4 X 3 X 2 CM
18-karat gold, 22-karat gold,
pink tourmaline; forged, set
PHOTO BY FXP PHOTOGRAPHY

Tom Munsteiner

Ring: Magic Eye | 2008

2.9 X 3 X 1 CM

Morganite, 18-karat yellow gold

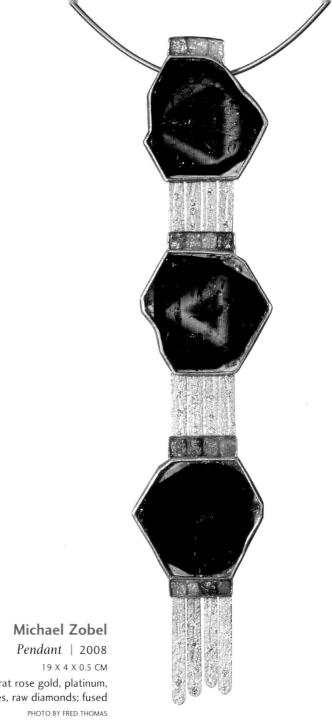

Michael Zobel
Pendant | 2008
19 X 4 X 0.5 CM
Sterling silver, 18-karat rose gold, platinum,
tourmalines, raw diamonds; fused
PHOTO BY FRED THOMAS

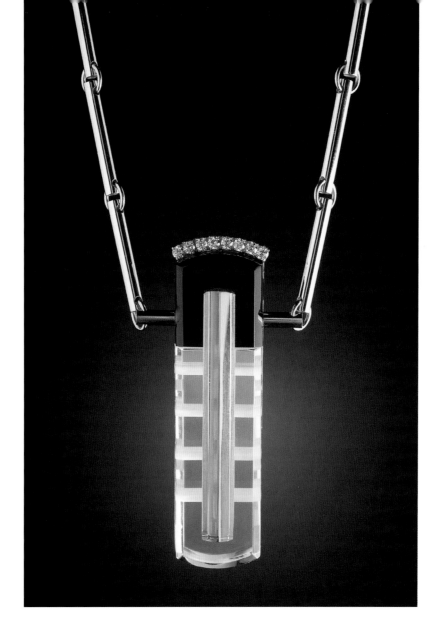

Linda MacNeil

Lucent Lines Necklace | 2005

5 X 2 X 1.3 CM

Vitrolite, clear glass, 14-karat
white gold, diamonds; polished

PHOTO BY BILL TRUSLOW

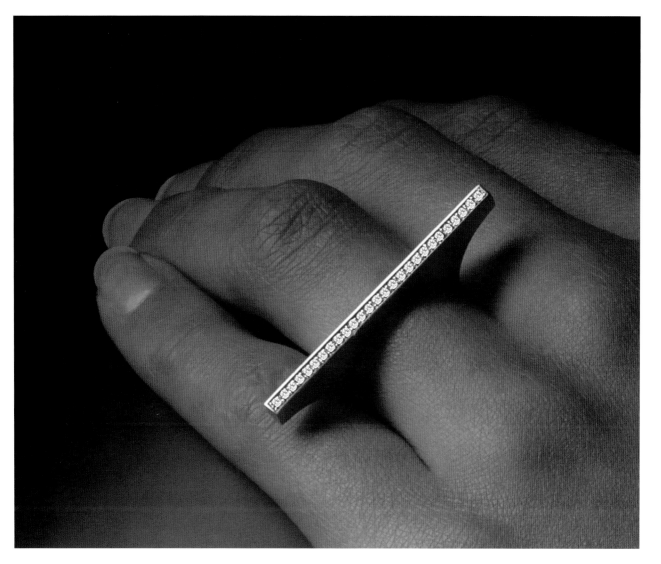

Steinbach-Condes
Ring | 2008
0.2 X 2.3 X 3.9 CM
18-karat palladium white gold, diamonds
PHOTO BY ARTISTS

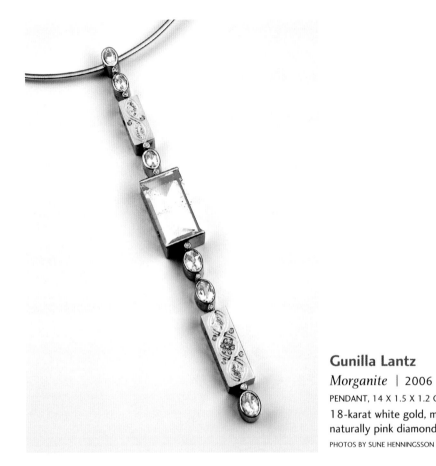

Gunilla Lantz

Morganite | 2006

PENDANT, 14 X 1.5 X 1.2 CM

18-karat white gold, morganites, naturally pink diamonds; engraved

PHOTOS BY SUNE HENNINGSSON

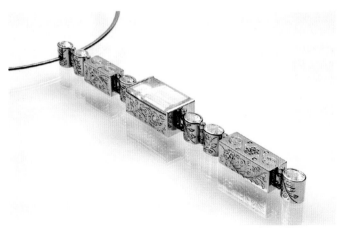

Claudio Pino

Ocean Blooms Collection | 2007

3.8 X 2.5 X 0.6 CM

Sterling silver, 14-karat gold, freshwater
pearls, pink quartz; fabricated, constructed

PHOTOS BY PHILOMÈNE LONGPRÉ

Jennifer Rabe Morin
Untitled | 2007
3.9 X 2.4 X 3.7 CM
18-karat white gold, amethyst, diamonds, mauve
agate cabochon; cast, pavé set, prong set
PHOTO BY GREGORY MORIN

Moritz Glik

Floating Chandelier Earrings | 2008

EACH, 7.5 X 4 X 0.5 CM

Diamonds, clear quartz crystal, 18-karat white gold

PHOTO BY PAULO FILGUEIRAS

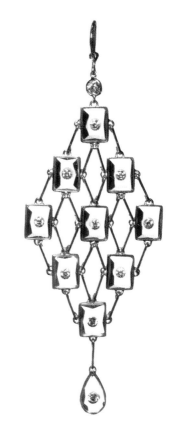

Jennifer Kellogg

Pavé Silhouette Diamond Ring | 2004

2 X 1 X 0.3 CM

14-karat white gold, diamonds

PHOTO BY LUIS ERNESTO SANTANA

157

Herman Hermsen
Mirror Brooch | 2008
DIAMETER, 5 CM
Acrylic, silver, zirconia
PHOTO BY ARTIST

Stephanie Jendis
Montblanc | 2005
6 X 3.5 X 2.5 CM
Ebony, ivory, amethyst, 18-karat gold
PHOTO BY ARTIST

Mary Esses
Pendant | 2006
19 X 4.5 X 1 CM
Amethysts, diamonds, iolites,
agate drops, white gold
PHOTO BY ARTIST

Gijs Bakker

Brooch Nr. 313: Marcos GT 1996 | 2001

4.8 X 8.3 X 2.6 CM

Sterling silver, amethyst, photograph, thermoplastic

PHOTO BY RIEN BAZEN

Ela Cindoruk

Round and Round | 2005

3.4 X 2.4 X 1.5 CM

Titanium, 18-karat gold, tourmaline;
formed, anodized, cold connected, cast

PHOTO BY ARTIST

Frédéric Braham
Cosmetic | 2007
2.9 X 5.9 X 0.8 CM
Computer-manipulated image, aluminum,
polyurethane varnish, polyester powder,
sterling silver,18-karat white gold, diamond
PHOTO BY ARTIST

Angela Eberhardt

The Ultimate Accessory | 2008

1.3 X 3.2 X 2.2 CM

Medical-grade acrylic, black diamonds, chocolate diamonds, blue sapphires, cubic zirconia

PHOTOS BY ARTIST

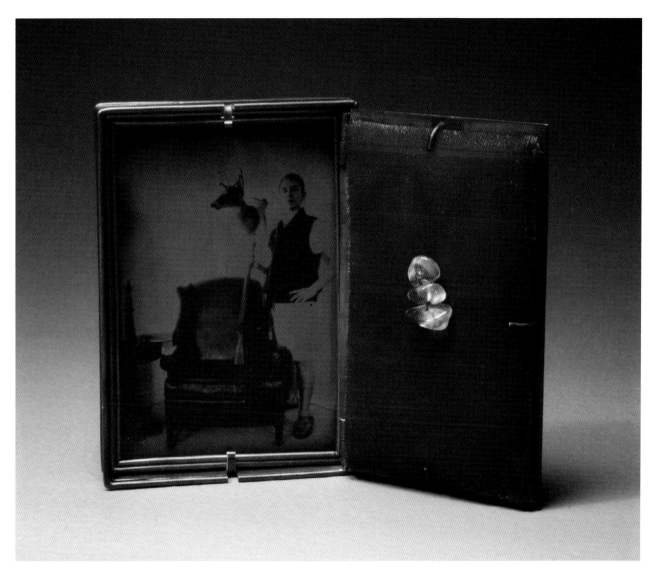

Andrew L. Kuebeck
Trophy Locket | 2007
10 X 6 X 2 CM
Copper, enamel, photograph, velvet, amber;
fabricated, die formed, hung, stitched
PHOTO BY ARTIST

Mauricio Serrano Jewelry
Facetas Ring | 2007
3 X 2 X 1.5 CM
Imbuia wood, rutilated quartz, white gold
PHOTO BY MAURICIO AVRAMOW

Cynthia Gale
Organic Cocktail Rings | 2008
EACH, 3 X 2.5 CM
Recycled sterling silver, mother-of-pearl, jade
PHOTO BY JOHN CURRY

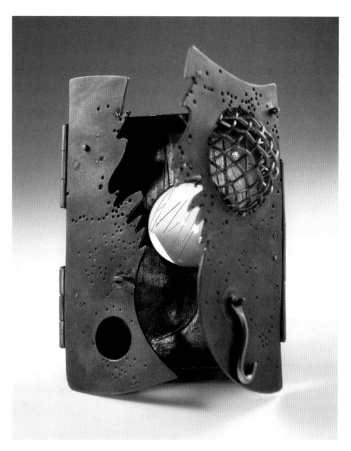

Kinga Rojek
Untitled | 2007

8 X 5.5 X 1.5 CM

Rutilated quartz, copper, brass,
bronze, sterling silver, gold leaf,
patina; fabricated, formed

PHOTOS BY KATHRYN OSGOOD

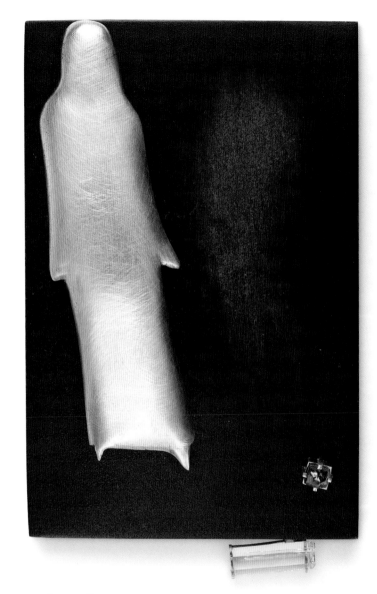

Kadri Mälk

Sudden Angel | 2006

7.8 X 4.3 X 1.4 CM

Cibatool, silver, white gold, aquamarine,
raw black diamond; carved, painted

PHOTO BY TIIT RAMMUL

Mary Hallam Pearse
Feeding Desire | 2008
8.9 X 6.4 X 1 CM
Sterling silver, aluminum, pearls, glass
PHOTO BY ARTIST

Anna Lorich

The Lamb and the Wolf Brooch | 2006

5.1 X 7.6 CM

Resin, plastic, pencil, 24-karat gold, 14-karat
gold, cushion-cut smoky quartz, ink

PHOTO BY ARTIST

Patty Smith

Cling | 2007

3.8 X 3.1 X 0.9 CM

Lake Superior basalt, biwa
pearl; drilled, sanded, set

PHOTO BY ARTIST

Mary Hallam Pearse

Tutti Frutti | 2008

7.6 X 6.4 X 1.3 CM

Sterling silver, aluminum, diamonds,
14-karat gold, glass

PHOTO BY ARTIST

Jane Dodd

Rabbit Leuchterweibchen Brooch | 2007

6 X 6.3 X 1.2 CM

Sterling silver, sapphire, ebony

PHOTO BY HARU SAMESHIMA

Gillian Hillerud

Paper Pendants | 2008

EACH, 3.8 X 3.8 X 1 CM

Silver, 14-karat gold, paper,
pearls, gemstones, thread

PHOTO BY VICKY LAM

April Higashi

Luna Ring | 2008

2.2 X 2.5 X 2.2 CM

Moonstone, 22-karat gold, 18-karat gold

PHOTO BY HAP SAKWA

Lauren Schott
*Eternity Wedding Band and Pretty
Baby Engagement Ring* | 2006
EACH, 0.4 X 0.4 CM
18-karat yellow gold, diamonds
PHOTO BY ARTIST

Claudia Steiner
2schwebende | 2008
2.5 X 1.5 X 2.7 CM
14-karat yellow gold, rutilated quartz
PHOTO BY STEFAN LIEWEHR

Alex Sepkus

Alex Sepkus Orchard Ring | 2008

LARGE STONE, 1.1 CM IN DIAMETER

18-karat rose gold, faceted round sapphires, diamonds

PHOTO BY ARUNAS KULIKAUSKAS

Mana Kehr
Muse | 2008
3.5 X 3.5 X 2.8 CM
Oval aquamarine cabochon,
18-karat gold, sterling silver, fine
silver; hand fabricated, milled
PHOTO BY JOSEF FISCHER

Marina Elenskaya
Untitled | 2007
5.5 X 2.5 X 3.5 CM
Ebony, crystal rock, silver
PHOTO BY FEDERICO CAVICCHIOLI

Akiko Kawayanagi of Mykonos
Nami | 2008
20 X 28 X 3 CM
Brass, fluorite, quartz, pearl; hand fabricated
PHOTO BY NOJYO

Claudia Endler

Mirror Aqua Pendant | 2007

3.8 X 2.5 X 1.9 CM

14-karat white gold, aquamarine, diamonds;
carved, cast, fabricated, laser welded

PHOTO BY BARRY BLAU

Suzan Rezac
Necklace | 2005
0.5 X 44 X 2 CM
Aquamarines, 18-karat green gold; constructed
PHOTO BY TOM VAN EYNDE

Cesar Lim

Shield Ring | 2007

6.4 X 2.5 X 3 CM

Aquamarines, tourmaline, diamonds, 18-karat white
gold, silver; hand forged, fabricated, oxidized, textured

PHOTO BY VLAD LAVROVSKY

Hema Malani

My Space | 2006

EACH EARRING, 2.9 X 1.4 X 1.5 CM; PENDANT, 3.4 X 1.5 X 1.2 CM

Diamonds, blue topaz, 18-karat white gold; bead set

PHOTO BY ARTIST

Robert Wander for Winc Creations

Untitled | 2005
18-karat yellow gold, aquamarines,
blue sapphires, chocolate diamonds

PHOTO BY NICOLE BROMSTAD

LAGOS
Glacier Luxe Rings | 2008
VARIOUS DIMENSIONS
Gemstones, diamonds, 18-karat gold, sterling silver
PHOTO BY KENNETH CAPPELLO

Jean-François Albert
Untitled | 2007

PINK MORGANITE, 2.8 X 2.2 CM;
NECKLACE, 50 CM LONG

Pink morganite, diamonds, 18-karat
yellow gold, 18-karat rose gold

PHOTO BY ARTIST

Anthony Nak

Tanzanite and Diamond Cuff in Platinum | 2006

5.5 X 6 X 5.6 CM

Platinum, tanzanite, diamonds; pavé set, frosted

PHOTO BY ARTIST

Mark Schneider

Neptune | 2008

3 X 2.5 X 1.6 CM

Platinum, yellow diamonds,
white diamonds, tourmaline

PHOTOS BY ARTIST

Ming Lampson

Hokusai Water Earrings | 2008

EACH, 7.6 X 1.3 X 0.2 CM

Brilliant-cut diamonds, marquise-cut
sapphires, enamel, 18-karat white
gold; handmade, carved, pavé set

PHOTO BY ARTIST

Suna Bros. Inc.

*Suna Award-Winning Floating
Tanzanite Necklace* | 2006

4.8 X 4.8 X 1 CM

Platinum, optical lens, tanzanite,
diamonds; constructed, cut, carved,
suspended, secured, drilled

DESIGNED BY MARIA CANALE
PHOTO BY HARMON GROUP

Carolina Bucci

Untitled | 2006

1.3 X 17.8 X 2 CM

18-karat gold, denim silk, white
diamonds, sapphires; woven

PHOTO BY ARTIST

Vicente Agor
Antarctica Collection: The Snow Globe Glacier Ring | 2008
3.4 X 2.6 X 2.7 CM
18-karat gold, rock crystal, Paraiba
tourmalines, diamonds; hand carved
PHOTO BY MIKE PFEFFER

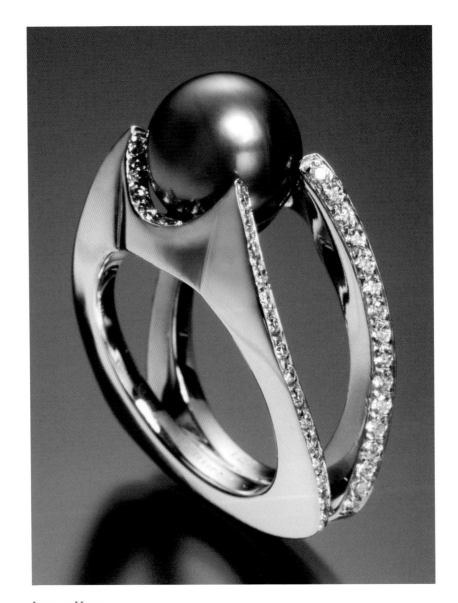

James Kaya

Birth | 2008

2.5 X 1.9 CM

18-karat white gold, black pearl,
diamonds; hand fabricated

PHOTO BY ROBERT DIAMANTE

Julia Fluker for Scott Reising Jewelers
Edwardian Ring | 2006
2.5 X 2.1 X 1.6 CM
Platinum, diamonds; cast, assembled
PHOTOS BY JAY BACHEMIN

Julia Lowther

Jet Heart Necklace | 2008

43 X 3.5 X 1.3 CM

Sterling silver, jet; hand fabricated, hand carved

JET CARVED BY DAVID VANCE HORSTE
PHOTO BY DANIEL VAN ROSSEN

Jennifer Yi

Symphony of Icicles | 2007

5.5 X 3.5 X 3 CM

Rock quartz, sterling silver; cast, hand fabricated,
soldered, hand carved, polished, set

PHOTO BY JENNY MCLAUGHLIN PHOTO

Jenna Brommer

Untitled | 2008

4 X 4 X 1.8 CM

Slate, pyrite, silver

PHOTO BY ARTIST

Michael Zobel

Brooch/Pendant—Broken Heart | 2008

6.2 X 4.5 X 0.5 CM

Sterling silver, 22-karat gold, platinum, tourmaline, diamonds

PHOTO BY FRED THOMAS

Jenna Brommer

Untitled | 2008

3.5 X 2.5 X 2.8 CM

Cobalt calcite, silver

PHOTOS BY ARTIST

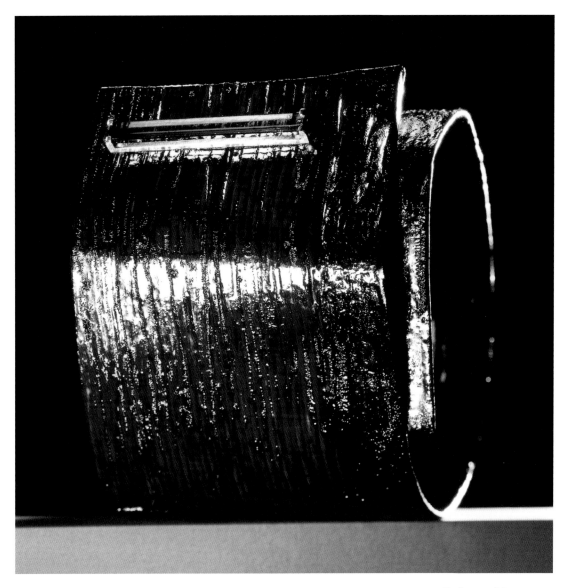

Salome Lippuner
Bracelet Bent Wood | 2004
6 X 8 X 6.5 CM
Urushi, fir, green tourmaline,
18-karat white gold
PHOTO BY XAVIER REBOUD

Jamie Fergus

Cut 'n Curl | 2007

7.5 X 4.5 X 0.9 CM

South Australian nephrite jade, Damascus
steel, 9-karat rose gold, silk

DAMASCUS STEEL BY SCOTT SANZ
PHOTO BY ARTIST

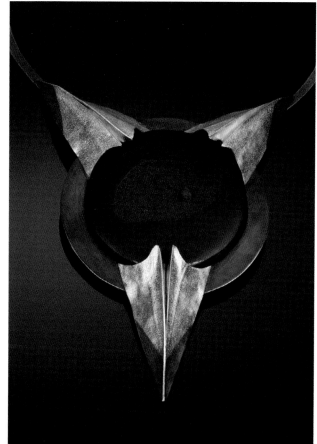

Judith Renstrom
Untitled | 2007

PENDANT, 16.5 X 11.5 X 1.5 CM
EACH EARRING, 9 X 2.3 X 1 CM

22-karat gold, fine silver, sterling
silver, black drusy; roller printed, kum
boo, fold formed, fabricated, oxidized

PHOTOS BY HUB WILLSON

Liaung Chung Yen

Past, Future, and Here I Am In Between | 2008

2.4 X 7 X 2 CM

18-karat yellow gold, 18-karat palladium white gold, quartz; fabricated, set

PHOTO BY ARTIST

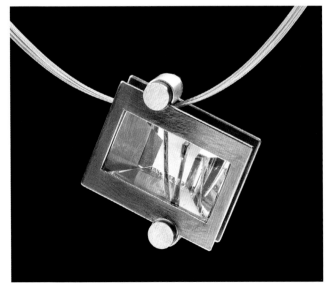

Pauline Barendse

Sticks in the Window | 2003

PENDANT, 4 X 3 X 1 CM

Silver, gold, rock crystal, tourmaline

PHOTO BY ROB GLASTRA

Todd Reed
Untitled | 2007

LARGEST, 1.4 X 0.2 CM

18-karat yellow gold, natural rose-cut
diamonds; hand forged, fabricated

PHOTO BY PRISCILLA MONTOYA

Chris Ploof

Meteorite Ring with Diamond | 2005

2.4 X 2.3 X 0.6 CM

18-karat yellow gold, diamond, meteorite; forged, fabricated

PHOTO BY ROBERT DIAMANTE

L. Sue Szabo

Emergence | 2007

4.4 X 3.2 X 3.2 CM

14-karat gold, 18-karat gold, straw topaz,
shibuishi; hand fabricated, back set, bezel set

PHOTO BY WES AIRGOOD

Lika Behar
24K Lava Lola Necklace | 2008
44.5 CM LONG
24-karat gold, lava stones; hand fabricated
PHOTO BY ARTIST

Linda Savineau
Rolling (Sea) Stones | 2008
21 X 21 X 2.5 CM
Raw amber, sterling silver; oxidized
PHOTO BY ARTIST

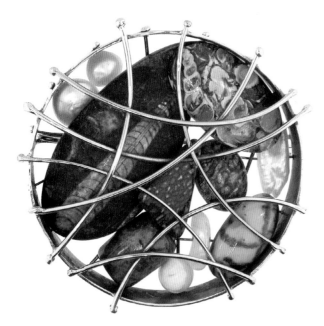

Carol Fugmann
Untitled | 2008
7.6 X 7.6 X 1.3 CM

Sterling silver, 14-karat gold, turitella agate, fossilized dinosaur bone, jasper, dendritic opal, coin, stick-cultured pearls, fossil, malachite, chrysocolla
PHOTO BY ARTIST

Andrzej Bielak
Play (Brooch) | 2007
5 X 5 CM
Sterling silver, raw Baltic amber; cut, cast
PHOTO BY BARBARA KANSKA-BIELAK

I like the flat setting used here

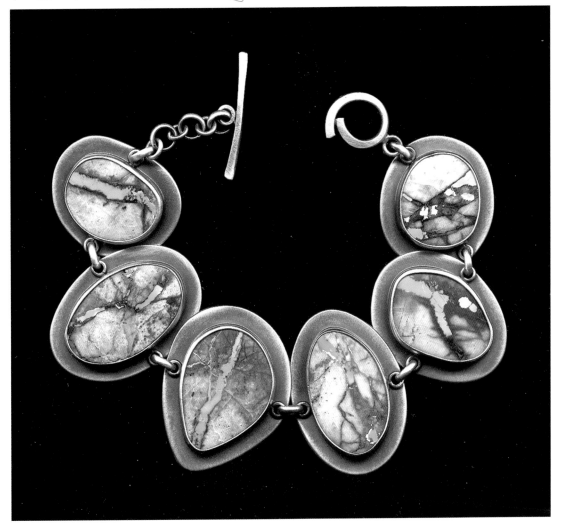

Kay Seurat
Royston Ribbon Turquoise | 2008
3.8 X 19 X 0.8 CM
Royston ribbon turquoise, sterling silver; hand fabricated
PHOTO BY ARTIST

Melinda Risk

Seeing Is Believing | 2008

2.5 X 2 CM

Oregon sunstone, diamonds, 22-karat gold, sterling silver, purpleheart, bloodwood; fabricated, carved

PHOTOS BY J. SCOTT PHOTOGRAPHY

Valerie Jo Coulson
Fiore Bracelet | 2008
10 X 10 X 1 CM
Sterling silver, red jasper, lace agate
PHOTOS BY CURTIS HALDY

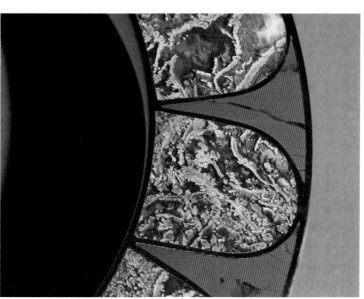

Ye Ram Jeon

Mango & Lime | 2007

LEFT, 4 X 10 X 10 CM; RIGHT, 4 X 4 X 4 CM

Serpentine, silver, Manao jade,
ebony, sterling silver

PHOTO BY KWANG CHOON PARK

Sandy Baker

Montoya | 2008

6 X 3 X 0.8 CM

Sterling silver, carnelian, black onyx,
coral, abalone, horn; handcrafted, inlaid

PHOTO BY KEN COX/KRONUS PHOTO

Johanna Dahm
Ring | 2008
DISC, 4.5 X 3.5 CM
Fine silver, steel wire, rough
black and yellow diamonds
PHOTO BY REINHARD ZIMMERMANN

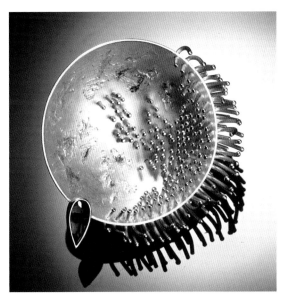

So Young Park
Sprouting Series | 2007
5 X 5 X 2 CM
18-karat yellow gold, tourmaline;
hammered, soldered, set
PHOTO BY GA RIM HONG

Rui Kikuchi

Natura Insolitus | 2008

3 X 2 X 2 CM

Silver, rough diamond, copper, gold
leaf; fabricated, cold connected

PHOTO BY ARTIST

Jung Eun Chang
Geometry from Nature | 2007
EACH, 8 X 4.5 X 4.5 CM
Sterling silver, hematite, garnet
PHOTO BY MYUNG-WOOK HUH

Stephanie Jendis
Vent | 2007
12 X 5 X 1 CM
Labradorite, found wood, steel cable, silver
PHOTO BY LUUK GEERTSEN

Karen Wuytens

Lava Ring 2 | 2007

4 X 1.2 X 2 CM

Silver, volcanic rock

PHOTO BY ARTIST

Christine J. Brandt

Lava | 2005

4 X 2.5 X 3 CM

African black ebony, vanadinite
crystals; hand carved

PHOTO BY MICHAEL BRANDT

Karl Fritsch

Die Tränen von Pandora | 2004

8 X 6 X 5 CM

Silver, various stones; oxidized

PHOTO BY ARTIST

Loretta Fontaine

Rusted Ring with Diamond | 2007

0.5 X 2.6 X 2.6 CM

14-karat gold, diamond, found object

PHOTO BY ARTIST

Serena Holm

Swing | 2007

7.2 X 6.7 X 1.5 CM

Silver, opal, raw diamond, zirconia, turquoise, glass, quartz, pearl, aquamarine, clock parts

PHOTO BY ARTIST

Kristina Glick Shank

Memory's Pieces: Three Watercolor Brooches | 2006

EACH LESS THAN 9 CM

Beach stones, shell fragments, pearl, shark's
tooth, snail shells, enamel, sterling silver, copper

PHOTO BY ARTIST

Zeb Chen

Pocket | 2008

4.5 X 3 X 0.8 CM

Silver, patina, agate

PHOTO BY ARTIST

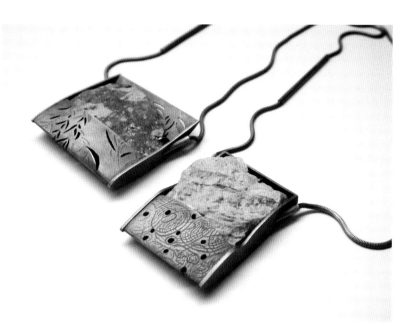

Giovanni Sicuro 'Minto'

MG 92—Ring | 2007

4 X 2.7 CM

Silver, enamel, quartz; hollow constructed

PHOTO BY ARTIST

Yuh-Shyuan Chen
Memory | 2004
2.7 X 2 X 1.9 CM
Silver, diamond; hand fabricated,
cold connected
PHOTO BY ARTIST

Selma Leal
Carpe Diem (n°01/05) | 2008
5 X 4 X 1 CM
Agate, diamonds, silver, gold, patina,
stainless steel; fabricated
PHOTO BY ARTIST

Caroline Gore
Untitled | 2007
1.3 X 2.5 X 3 CM
Raw diamond, 18-karat gold
PHOTO BY ARTIST

Selma Leal
Slow Down | 2008
8 X 6 X 1 CM
Tiger's eye, aquamarine, diamonds, silver,
patina, gold, stainless steel; fabricated
PHOTO BY ARTIST

Andrew Costen

Aqua Argentum | 2008

50 CM LONG

Aquamarine, sterling silver rondelles; handcrafted, textured

PHOTO BY CARLA WILSON

Hedvig Westermark
Smide och Form
PENDANT, 4 X 4.5 CM
Silver, gold, coral, aquamarine
PHOTO BY HANS BJURLING

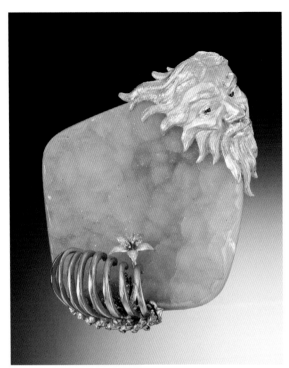

Kim Eric Lilot

Searching for Solace Brooch | 2008

6 X 4.5 X 2 CM

Platinum, 14-karat, 18-karat, and 22-karat yellow, white, and green gold, botroydal drusy agate, rubies, enamel; lost wax cast, hand fabricated, hand fired

PHOTO BY HAP SAKWA

Vikki Kassioras

Chiron | 2004

3 X 2 X 1.5 CM

18-karat yellow gold, carnelian;
hand-carved intaglio

CARVED BY S. KOLIOPOULOU
PHOTO BY TERENCE BOGUE

Mary Watson

Earth Spirit Guides | 2008

LARGEST, 7.6 X 5 X 1.3 CM

Sterling silver, Mojave Desert jasper, green jasper,
tagua, coral, peridot, lake stone bases; carved

PHOTO BY LARRY SANDERS

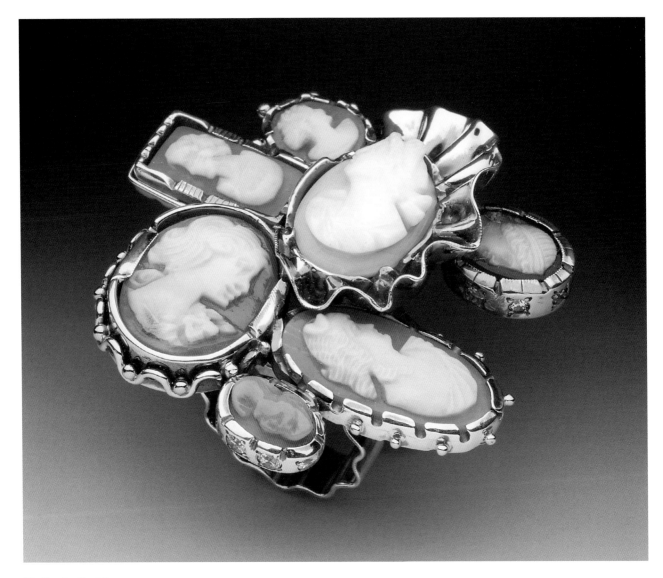

Kelly L. Robinson

Cameo Ring | 2008

3.2 X 4.7 X 4.9 CM

Sterling silver, 18-karat yellow gold, white cubic zirconia, cameo stones, patina; fabricated, corrugated, bead set, bezel set, soldered

PHOTO BY DON CASPER

Shay Lahover
Untitled | 2007

6 X 6 CM

18-karat gold, 22-karat gold, 24-karat gold, coral,
peridot, pearl, diamonds, labradorite; handmade

PHOTO BY YOSSI ZWECKER

Loretta Fontaine

Bishop's Lane Series: Zinnia Necklace | 2004

3 X 4.4 X 0.4 CM

22-karat gold, sterling silver, color photographs, mica,
aquamarine cabochons, sea glass, shells, barnacle,
tourmaline beads, patina; hand fabricated, granulated

PHOTO BY TABOO STUDIO

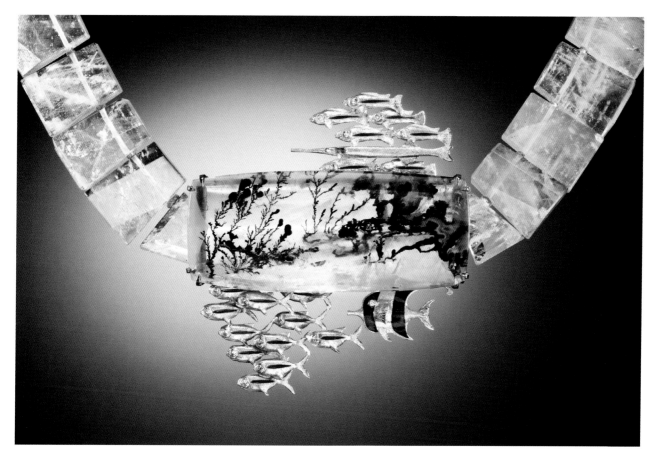

Kim Eric Lilot

Sea Life Necklace | 2008

45 X 7.2 X 2 CM

18-karat yellow, white, and red gold, dendritic
quartz, aquamarine, diamonds, enamel; lost
wax cast, hand fabricated, hand fired

CARVED BY DIETER LORENZ
PHOTO BY HAP SAKWA

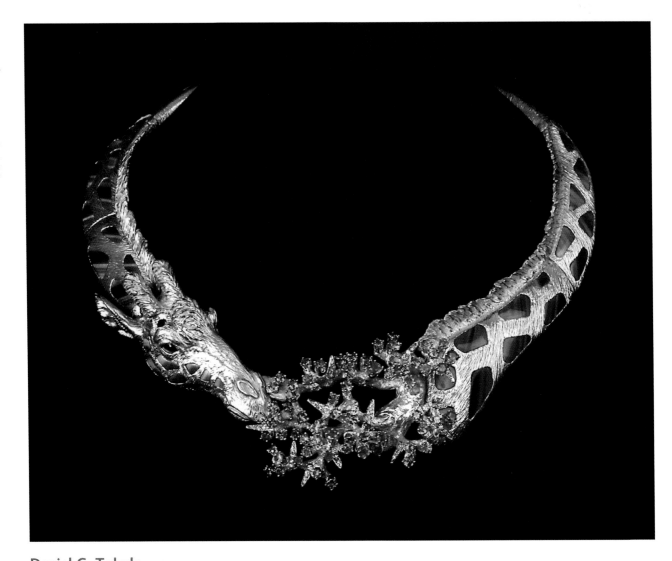

Daniel C. Toledo

The Jeweled Giraffe | 2004

16.5 X 17.7 CM

Platinum, 18-karat yellow gold, 22-karat yellow gold, tiger's
eye, alexandrite cat's eye, emeralds, tsavorites, diamonds

PHOTO BY ARTIST

Pandora Barthen
Heart of Africa | 2008
8.6 X 7.6 CM

18-karat yellow gold, enamel, rose-cut
diamonds, Lightening Ridge black opal,
rubies; lost wax cast, plique-à-jour

PHOTO BY LEE WOOLDRIDGE

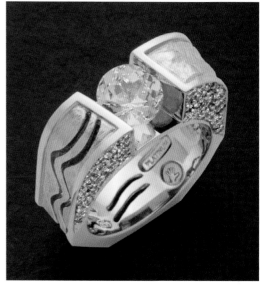

Marc Stiglitz

Journey So Far 10-Year Anniversary Ring | 2008

2.6 X 2.2 X 0.9 CM

Platinum, natural yellow sapphire, round ideal-cut
diamonds; hand carved, lost wax cast, hand textured

PHOTOS BY GEORGE POST PHOTOGRAPHY

George Sawyer
Winter Koi | 2007
EACH, 2.5 X 2.5 X 1 CM
14-karat gray gold, fine silver, white
diamonds, fancy intense yellow diamonds
PHOTO BY ARTIST

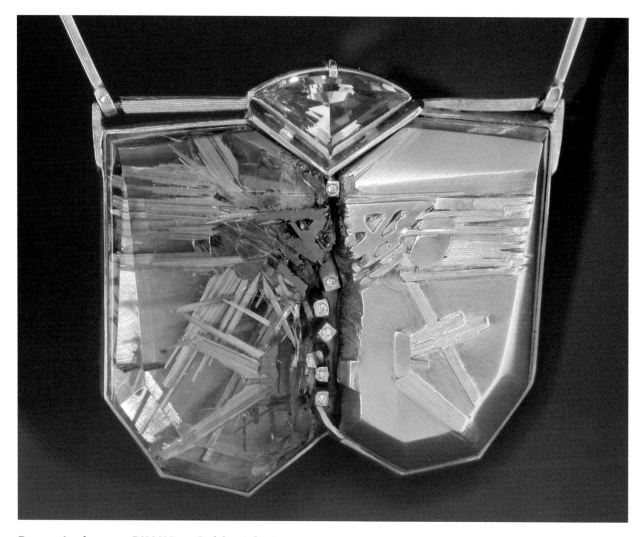

Bruce Anderson, RW Wise Goldsmiths Inc.

18K/Platinum Rutilated Quartz Gem Sculpture Pendant | 2002

4.8 X 5.1 X 1 CM

18-karat yellow gold, palladium white gold,
platinum, rutilated quartz, yellow beryl, diamonds

RUTILATED QUARTZ GEM SCULPTURE BY GLENN LEHRER
PHOTO BY BETH HUMPHREY

Hagen Gamisch
Aedes Sol | 2008
4 X 4.7 X 2.4 CM
14-karat gold, smoky quartz; CAD, sandcast
PHOTO BY ARTIST

Lilly Fitzgerald

Multi-Colored Sapphire Necklace | 2008

EACH STONE, 3.8 TO 5.1 CM

22-karat gold, sapphires; hand fabricated, cast

PHOTO BY HAP SAKWA

Andrea denElzen

Interlocking Rings | 2008

EACH, 2.7 X 1 X 2.2 CM

18-karat white gold, 18-karat yellow gold,
orange sapphire, cinnamon diamonds

PHOTO BY PAUL AMBTMAN

ZIL

Beatriz Earrings | 2006

EACH, 7 X 2 X 0.5 CM

Yellow citrines, orange citrines, 18-karat gold

PHOTO BY EDUARDO CONTE

Lisa Krikawa

Juicy Liqueur | 2007

3 X 2.1 X 0.8 CM

22-karat rose gold, 18-karat rose gold,
22-karat yellow gold, 18-karat white
gold, sapphires; mokume gane, pavé set

PHOTOS BY HAP SAKWA

Julez Bryant
Star Necklace | 2008
14-karat rose gold, fancy cognac diamonds
PHOTO BY ANDREA ROTENBERG

Mads Kornerup

Bracelet 1 | 2008

1 X 6.5 X 6.5 CM

Nylon string, pink argyle diamond pavé ball,
white diamond pavé ball, black diamond pavé
ball, 18-karat white gold balls; macraméd

PHOTO BY FREDERIK LINDSTROM

Aaron Henry Furlong

Diamond Arbor Rings | 2002

SMALLEST, 2.1 X 2.1 X 0.2 CM; LARGEST, 2.3 X 2.3 X 0.4 CM

18-karat rose gold, 19.2-karat yellow gold,
platinum, diamonds, bright-cut accents; bead set

PHOTO BY ARTIST

Pamela Froman

The Dreamer | 2007

PENDANT, 5 X 3.7 X 0.7 CM; CHAIN, 45.7 CM LONG

18-karat pink, white, and green crushed gold, round brilliant-cut white diamonds, natural grey rose-cut diamond, natural grey diamond briolette, rough grey diamond beads

PHOTOS BY JAY LAWRENCE GOLDMAN, JLG PHOTO

Suzy Landa
Flip-Top Bangle Bracelet | 2008
6.4 X 7 X 3.2 CM
18-karat rose gold, white topaz, diamond
PHOTO BY TARA DIGIOVANNI

Moritz Glik
Kaleidoscope Ring | 2008
2.8 X 2.8 X 0.5 CM
Diamonds, double white sapphires,
18-karat yellow gold
PHOTO BY PAULO FILGUEIRAS

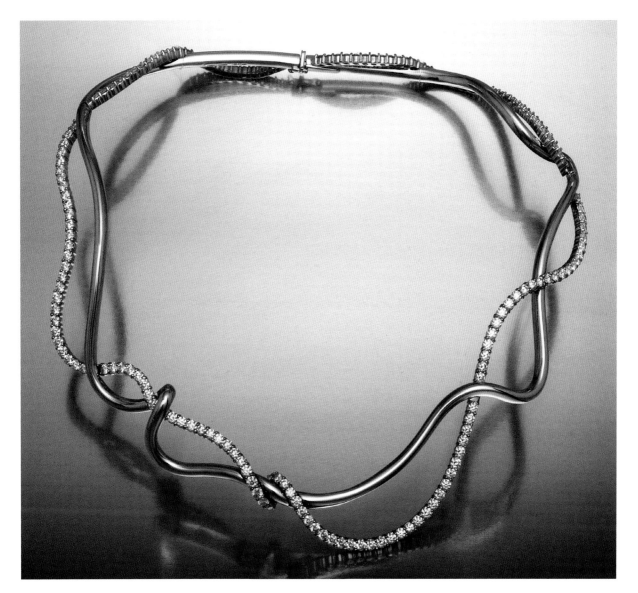

Diana Vincent

Wind Necklace | 2003

15.2 X 15.2 X 3.2 CM

Platinum, 18-karat yellow gold, round
brilliant-cut diamonds; handmade

PHOTO BY DIANA VINCENT INC.

Susan Helmich

Untitled | 2005

8 X 4 CM

Morganite, diamonds, 18-karat gold, platinum; fabricated

MORGANITE CUT BY TOM MUNSTEINER
PHOTO BY JOSH HELMICH

Robert Wander for Winc Creations
Untitled | 2008
PENDANT, 8.1 CM LONG
Golden beryl, chocolate diamonds, white diamonds
PHOTO BY NICOLE BROMSTAD

245

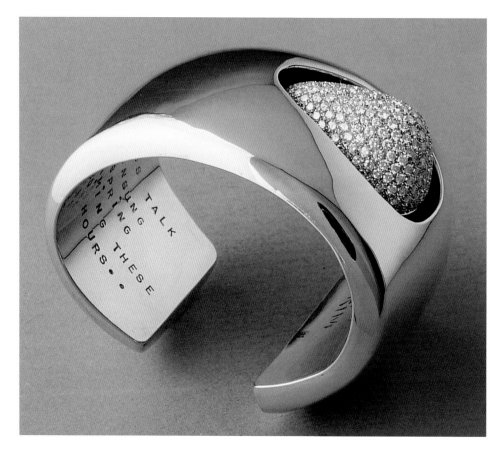

Kim Rawdin

For Joan | 1998

5 X 6.4 X 5.7 CM

18-karat gold, diamonds; fabricated,
hollow formed, soldered, cut, pavé set

PHOTO BY ARTIST

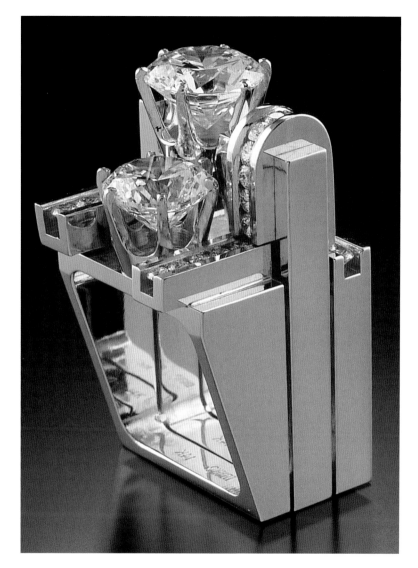

Robert C. Trisko
14-Karat Gold Amusement
Park Ring of Diamonds | 2005
3.8 X 1.9 X 2.5 CM
Diamonds
PHOTO BY LARRY SANDERS

Alex Sepkus

Alex Sepkus Sea Grass Ring | 2008

LARGE STONE, 1.1 X 0.9 X 0.5 CM

18-karat yellow gold, diamonds, oval faceted red spinel

PHOTO BY ARUNAS KULIKAUSKAS

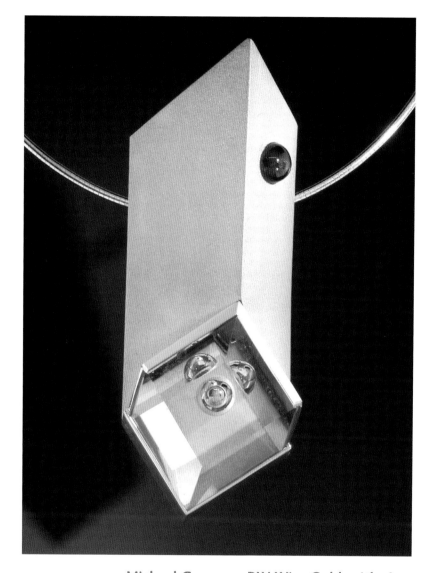

Michael Corneau, RW Wise Goldsmiths Inc.

18K Gem Sculpture Pin/Pendant | 2008

7.3 X 2.7 X 1.4 CM

18-karat gold, smoky quartz, orange
sunstone cabochon; sandblasted

SMOKY QUARTZ GEM SCULPTURE BY TOM MUNSTEINER
PHOTO BY BETH HUMPHREY

Steinbach-Condes

Ring | 2007

2.2 X 2.2 X 2.4 CM

18-karat yellow gold, orange sapphire

PHOTO BY ARTISTS

Dorothy N. Friedberg
Golden Eye Ring | 2007
2 X 2.5 X 3.5 CM
18-karat gold, madera citrine; carved, cast
PHOTO BY ARTIST

Ela Cindoruk
In Between | 2005
2.7 X 2.9 X 1 CM
18-karat gold, rutilated quartz; formed
PHOTO BY ARTIST

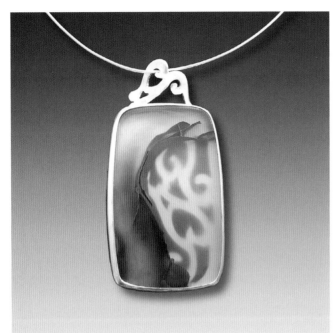

Diane Weimer
Untitled | 2006
5.8 X 3 X 0.5 CM
Sterling silver, fine silver, Mexican agate
PHOTO BY ARTIST

Adri Kaminski
Héstia | 2007
2.7 X 2.2 X 4.1 CM
Silver, quartz
PHOTO BY ARTIST

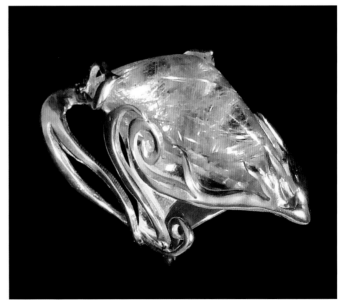

Patrick Murphy
Untitled | 2008

2.3 X 1.5 X 3 CM

18-karat gold, dendritic agate, citrine,
brown diamond; hand fabricated

PHOTO BY COREY MORSE

Mary Ann Buis

Azula | 2008

1.5 X 38 X 0.7 CM

Lapis lazuli beads, 19-karat white gold, 18-karat yellow gold,
magnetic clasp, rutilated quartz, round brilliant-cut diamonds;
handcrafted, channel set, custom cut, pavé set

PHOTO BY CARLA WILSON

Lucy Godoroja
Pleiades | 2008
45 CM LONG
Boulder opal, 18-karat
yellow gold, sterling silver
PHOTO BY RICHARD WEINSTEIN

Jeffrey Kaphan

Turquoise Earrings | 1996

EACH, 3.8 X 3.8 CM

Turquoise, chrome tourmaline, freshwater pearl
drops, 14-karat yellow gold; cast, fabricated

PHOTO BY PERRY JOHNSON/IMAGICA

Thomas Herman
Turquoise Oak Brooch | 2008
6.6 X 3.7 X 0.8 CM
18-karat gold, Chinese turquoise; cast,
fabricated, chased, engraved, saw pierced
PHOTO BY ALLEN BRYAN

Melinda Risk

The Garden | 2008

3.7 X 1.8 CM

Chalcedony, pink sapphire, 22-karat gold, sterling silver; fabricated, cast

PHOTOS BY J. SCOTT PHOTOGRAPHY

Boline Strand

Punica Granatum Necklace | 2008

PENDANT, 4.4 X 1.9 X 1.9 CM;
NECK RING, 14 CM IN DIAMETER

Faceted ruby beads, 18-karat gold;
hand fabricated, beaded

PHOTO BY TOM MILLS

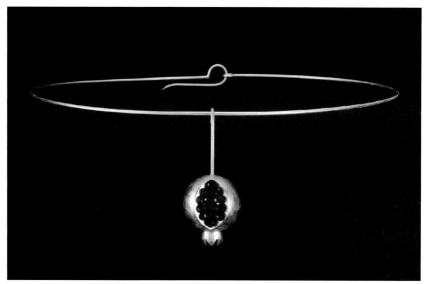

Jessica Fields

Lotus Teardrop Earrings with Tourmaline | 2007

EACH, 4 X 1.8 X 0.3 CM

18-karat yellow gold, pink tourmaline
cabochons; cast, hand fabricated

PHOTO BY ARTIST

Jessica Fields

18K Gold & Gemstone Ring Pile | 2008

VARIOUS DIMENSIONS

18-karat gold, sapphire, tourmaline, diamond; cast, hand set

PHOTO BY ARTIST

Karin Worden
Anemone | 2008

7.6 X 6.4 X 1.3 CM

Sterling silver, 22-karat gold, 24-karat gold, 18-karat palladium
white gold, 18-karat yellow gold, chalcedony, purple sapphires

PHOTO BY HAP SAKWA

Amy Cannon

Bouquet Ring with Seven Screw-On Tops | 2007

LARGEST TOP, 1.5 X 2.3 X 2.3 CM

18-karat yellow gold, 14-karat yellow gold, sterling silver, sapphire, cubic zirconium, peridot, rhodolite garnet, raven's wing freshwater pearl, peach freshwater pearl, lemon quartz

PHOTO BY RICHARD WALKER

Ann L. Lumsden
Bellybutton Ornament | 2007

6.1 CM IN DIAMETER

18-karat white gold, 18-karat yellow gold,
silk flowers, diamond; cast, constructed

PHOTOS BY ARTIST

Asato Phillip Tanaka

To Shizuko | 2007

5 X 2.5 X 2.5 CM

Champagne cork, diamonds, silver; mixed-media
assemblage, soldered, pierced, bent

PHOTOS BY ARTIST

Jan Matthesius

Untitled (Ring) | 1992

3 X 2.5 X 2 CM

Tantalum, gold, amethyst, diamond

PHOTO BY ROB GLASTRA

Wes Airgood

Bomb and Diamonds Ring | 2008

3.2 X 3.2 X 2.5 CM

Sterling silver, onyx, diamonds, steel

PHOTOS BY ARTIST

Jan Matthesius
Untitled (Ring) | 1981
3 X 2.5 X 1.5 CM
Gold, morganite
PHOTO BY ROB GLASTRA

Rui Kikuchi
Insect Egg Series (Laccotrephes japonensis) | 2008
4 X 3 X 2 CM
Silver, pearl, gold leaf; fabricated
PHOTO BY ARTIST

Sarah Keay
Ruby Bangle | 2008
14 X 12 X 2.5 CM
9-karat gold, rubies, monofilament,
enamel; bobbin knitted, hand fabricated
PHOTO BY ARTIST

Jung Eun Chang

Pongdang Pongdang | 2007

EACH, 3.5 X 2.5 X 1 CM

Sterling silver, amethyst, rutilated
quartz, aquamarine, moldavite

PHOTO BY MYUNG-WOOK HUH

Mary Esses

Pendant | 2006

11 X 3 X 1 CM

Smoky quartz, diamonds, rhodolites, rubies

PHOTO BY ARTIST

Tomonori Hakase

Nude | 2008

2.2 X 2.7 X 0.8 CM

Ruby, 14-karat white gold

PHOTO BY ARTIST

Kendra Roberts

Seascape at Sunrise | 2005

24.1 CM IN DIAMETER; 61 CM LONG

Turquoise, lapis lazuli, pink rhodonite, mother-of-pearl, oyster shell, ivory, apple green turquoise, sterling silver; inlaid

PHOTO BY RALPH GABRINER

Anette Rack

Ring: One Size Fits All | 2007

3 X 2.5 X 1.5 CM

Aquamarine, 18-karat gold, hook-and-loop tape; dyed

PHOTO BY GÜNTHER DÄCHERT

Claire Townsend

Unusual Beauty | 2007

2 X 1.5 X 1 CM

Sterling silver, 18-karat yellow gold, drusy chrysocolla

PHOTO BY MIKE GRAY

Salome Lippuner
Ring Coco | 2007
4.5 X 6 X 2.5 CM
Urushi, coconut, chloromelanite, sterling silver
PHOTO BY XAVIER REBOUD

Marianne Schliwinski
Il Giardino | 2007
4.3 X 6.5 X 1.2 CM
Fine silver, palladium, gold, glass, rock
crystal, fluorite, paper; mounted
PHOTO BY JÜRGEN EICKHOFF

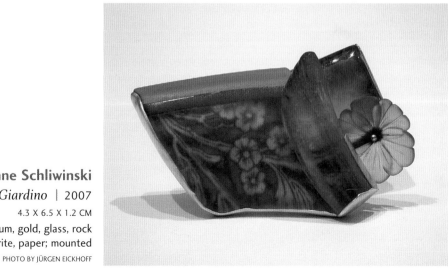

Satoru W. Bauman
Untitled | 2007
4.8 X 1.7 X 0.7 CM
Wood, 18-karat gold, stainless steel,
diamonds, rubies; turned, cut, riveted
PHOTO BY ARTIST

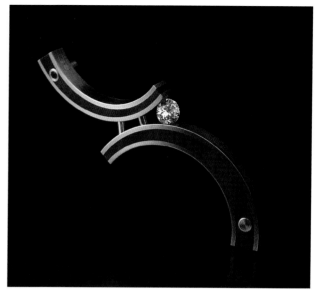

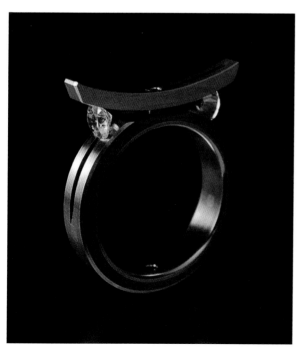

Satoru W. Bauman
Untitled | 2007
2.5 X 2.2 X 0.5 CM
Wood, 18-karat gold, stainless steel,
diamonds, rubies; turned, cut, riveted
PHOTO BY ARTIST

Melinda Risk

Nest Egg | 2008

3.4 X 2 CM

Turquoise, blue diamond, 22-karat
gold, sterling silver; fabricated, cast

PHOTO BY J. SCOTT PHOTOGRAPHY

Emily C. Johnson
Untitled | 2008

EACH, 5 X 0.8 X 0.4 CM

Sterling silver, 18-karat yellow gold, rutilated
quartz cabochons, patina; hand fabricated

PHOTO BY KALIN KAUPPILA

Wesley Glebe
Untitled | 2006

0.4 X 2.4 X 0.3 CM

Titanium, turquoise, diamonds, 14-karat white gold;
cold connected, lathe turned, tube set, riveted

PHOTO BY ARTIST

Jacob Albee

Obelisk Necklace | 2008

3.8 X 2.3 X 0.5 CM

Indicolite tourmaline, 22-karat, 18-karat, and 14-karat
gold, Gibeon meteorite, diamonds; hand fabricated, etched

INDICOLITE TOURMALINE CUT BY DAVID BRACKNA
PHOTO BY ALEX WILLIAMS

Zamama Metal Arts Studio

Rings | 2008

EACH, 2.5 X 1.8 X 2.5 CM

Sterling silver, jade

PHOTO BY ARTIST

Erik Stewart

Moon Cheese | 2006

3 X 2.1 X 0.3 CM

Sterling silver, rough diamond

PHOTO BY ARTIST

Pat Pruitt
Untitled | 2007
2.5 X 2.5 X 0.4 CM
Stainless steel, industrial diamonds; machined,
compression set, chiseled, diamond-cut textured
PHOTO BY ARTIST

Jane Bowden
Wrapped Ring | 2006
2.9 X 2.6 X 0.8 CM
18-karat white gold, 18-karat yellow gold, princess-cut
diamonds; hand fabricated, stone setting, threaded
PHOTO BY GRANT HANCOCK

Niyati Haft
New-Found Land | 2007

3.5 X 3.7 X 0.6 CM

22-karat, 18-karat, and 14-karat gold, sterling silver, card-
board, aquamarine; hammered, soldered, constructed, set

PHOTO BY KASHI-DIGITAL DESIGN

Roberto Fioravanti

Untitled | 2007

3.3 X 2.1 X 0.8 CM

Sterling silver, 18-karat yellow gold, moonstone, emeralds; forged, soldered, textured, set

PHOTO BY JOHN C. WATSON

Pat Pruitt
Untitled | 2007
7 X 3 X 5 CM
Stainless steel, industrial diamonds; machined, hydraulic press
formed, compression set, sanded, bead blasted, polished
PHOTO BY ARTIST

Fran Grinels

Rorschach Test #1 | 2006

2.5 X 2.9 X 2.9 CM

White diamond, brass, sterling silver;
fabricated, tube set, oxidized

PHOTO BY SAM GRINELS

Bruce Anderson
Brooch B2002.2 | 2002
5.5 X 6 X 1.3 CM
Sterling silver, 18-karat yellow gold,
lapis lazuli, pearls; constructed, fused
PHOTO BY RALPH GABRINER

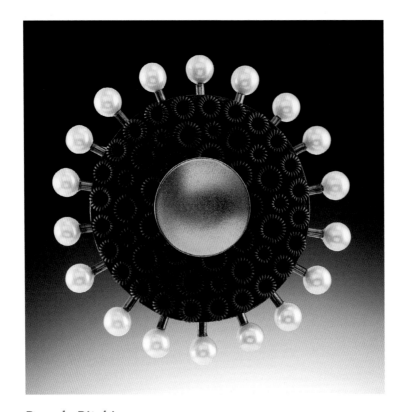

Pamela Ritchie
Norwegian Soul Brooch | 2007
4.8 X 4.8 X 1.2 CM
Sterling silver, 18-karat gold, pearls
PHOTO BY PERRY JACKSON

Todd Reed

Circular Rose-Cut Brooch | 2006

7.6 X 7 X 0.7 CM

Antique rose-cut diamonds, raw diamond cubes, 18-karat
yellow gold, silver, patina; hand forged, fabricated

PHOTO BY ARTIST

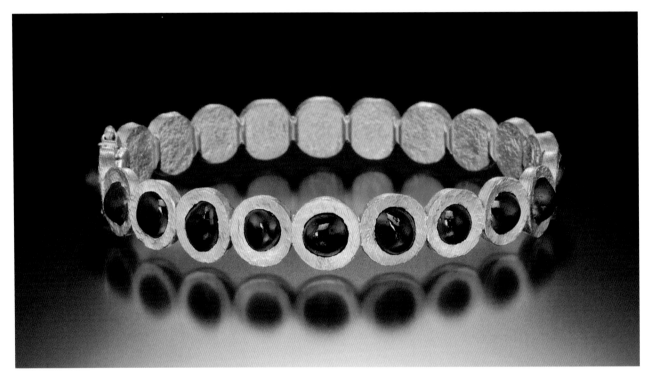

Devta Doolan

Black Diamond Cabochon Bracelet | 2007

9 X 7 X 1 CM

24-karat gold, platinum, black diamonds; fabricated

PHOTO BY HAP SAKWA

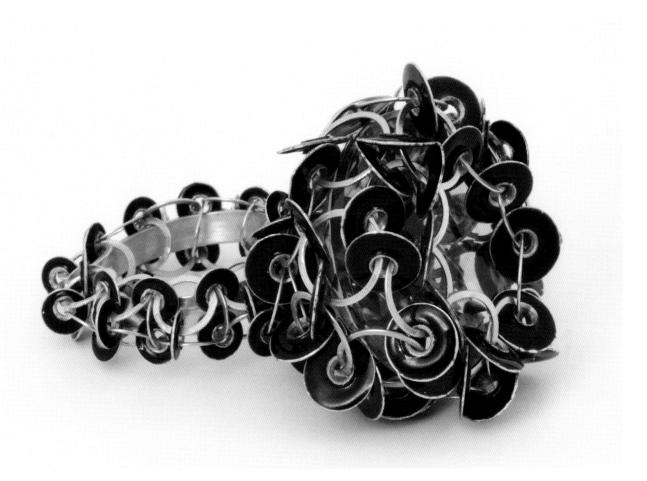

Ralph Bakker
Solitaire 4 | 2008
6 X 3.5 X 3.5 CM
Gold, silver, enamel, lemon quartz
PHOTOS BY ARTIST

Todd Reed

Untitled | 2007

1.2 X 1.3 CM

18-karat gold, diamonds;
hand forged, fabricated

PHOTO BY HAP SAKWA

Keith Lewis
Mica Bangle | 2008
12 X 12 X 1.5 CM
Mica, freshwater pearls, 23-karat
gold leaf; layered, shellacked
PHOTO BY RALPH GABRINER

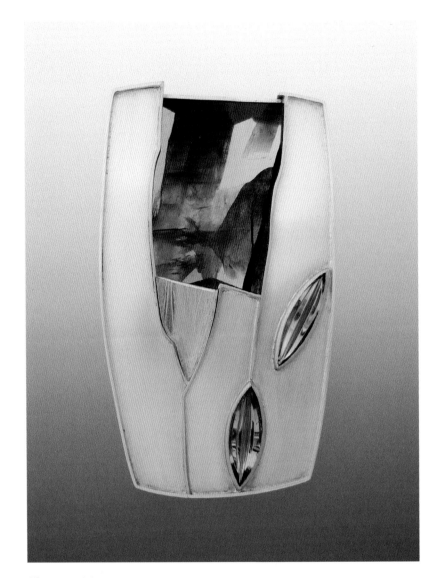

Eleanor Moty

Autumnal Veil Brooch | 2008

7.2 X 4.3 X 1.2 CM

Sterling silver, 22-karat gold, 18-karat gold, quartz, iron oxide, citrines

QUARTZ BY HERMAN PETRY
CITRINES BY TOM MUNSTEINER
PHOTO BY ARTIST

Thomas Herman

Indonesian Plume Agate Brooch | 2008

4.3 X 4.3 X 0.8 CM

18-karat gold, Indonesian plume agate, diamonds;
turned, cast, chased, engraved, saw pierced

PHOTO BY ALLEN BRYAN

German Kabirski
Ring: Winter | 2008
2.3 X 2.8 X 0.8 CM
18-karat gold, white diamonds, calcite, ruby
PHOTO BY ARTIST

Eun Jung Kim
Bamboo (Brooch) | 2007
5.7 X 2.6 X 0.8 CM
18-karat gold, 24-karat gold, jadeite,
diamond; cast, carved, pavé set
PHOTO BY STUDIO MUNCH

Marianne Hunter

The Universe Sings | 2006

6.4 X 26.7 X 0.8 CM

Grisaille enamels, pure gold foil, pure silver foil, quartz,
pyrite, epidote, iron, diamonds, citrine, phrenite,
24-karat gold, 14-karat gold; fabricated, engraved

PHOTO BY HAP SAKWA

Nicole Uurbanus

Night (Year of the Rings) | 2002

2.5 X 2.1 X 1.8 CM

18-karat gold, azurite; lost wax cast

PHOTO BY ROGER PANHAN

Petra Class

Blue Yellow Stars | 2008

3.2 X 3.2 X 1.3 CM

Diamonds, aquamarines, sapphires, topaz,
pearl, 22-karat gold, 18-karat gold; fabricated

PHOTO BY HAP SAKWA

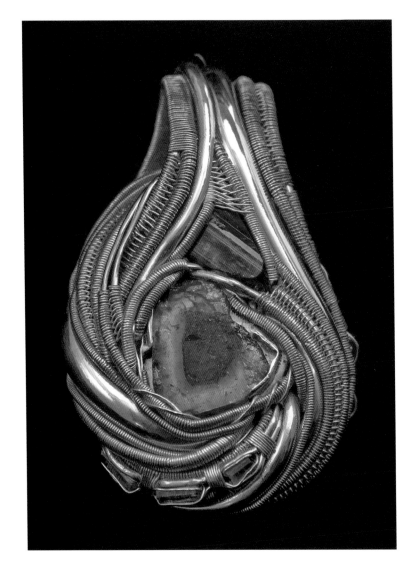

Sarah Williamson

Incident at Gate 7 | 2006

5.1 X 3.2 X 1.3 CM

24-karat yellow gold, 22-karat red gold, 18-karat
green gold, 18-karat white gold, Paraiba watermelon
tourmaline slice, tanzanite crystal, emerald crystals,
spinel crystals; bezel set, cold fusion

PHOTO BY ADRIEN ROBERT

Julie Lynn Romanenko for Just Jules, LLC
Waterfall | 2005
6 X 2.5 X 0.3 CM

14-karat gold, Australian boulder opals, Brazilian green
tourmaline, diamonds, freshwater pearls; hand fabricated

PHOTO BY GEORGE POST

Marianne Hunter
Could the Night Be More Beautiful? | 2008
27.9 X 3.2 X 1.3 CM

Enamel, diamonds, sapphires, emerald,
apatite, lapis lazuli, kyanite, benetoite,
24-karat gold, 14-karat gold, platinum-silver

PHOTO BY GEORGE POST

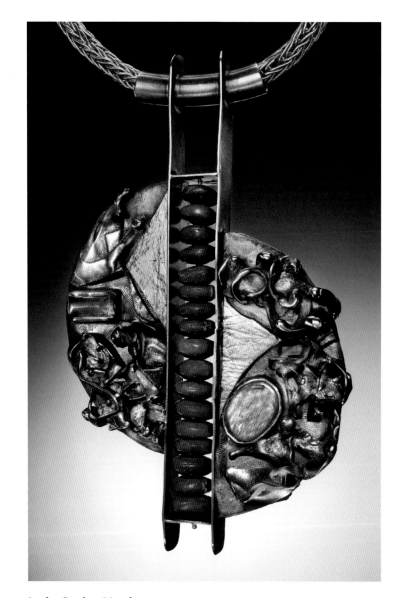

Judy Staby Hoch

Double Double Bead | 2008

8.9 X 5.7 X 0.9 CM

Sterling silver, 18-karat gold, lapis lazuli, quartz, labradorite;
mokume gane, hollow formed, fabricated

PHOTO BY RALPH GABRINER

Judith Kaufman
Untitled | 2009
5.7 X 5.7 X 0.6 CM
Columbian sapphire crystal, diamonds, sapphire, 18-karat
yellow gold, 22-karat yellow gold; cut, polished
PHOTO BY HAP SAKWA

Mary Watson

Globeberries | 2007

6.4 X 6.4 X 1.3 CM

Sterling silver, enamel, copper, black
jasper, lake stone base; torch fired

Sessin Durgham

Heavy Bracelet | 2007

10.2 X 2.5 CM

Silver, 22-karat gold, black jade, chrysoprase, dinosaur
bone, green turquoise; roller printed, hand carved

PHOTO BY JERRY ANTHONY

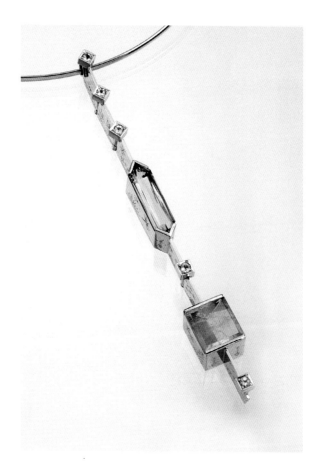

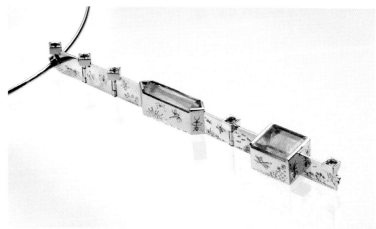

Gunilla Lantz

Untitled | 2006

PENDANT, 13.5 X 1.4 X 1.2 CM

18-karat white gold, yellow beryl, chrysoberyls; engraved

PHOTOS BY SUNE HENNINGSSON

Andrew Costen

Passions Flame | 2007

EACH, 3 X 2.2 X 0.6 CM

19-karat white gold, natural orange fire opals, round tsavorite garnets, round brilliant-cut diamonds; handcrafted, channel set

PHOTO BY CARLA WILSON

Patrick Murphy

Untitled | 2008

2 X 1.3 X 3 CM

14-karat gold, Ray Mine chrysocolla,
spinel, garnet; hand fabricated

PHOTO BY COREY MORSE

Shay Lahover
Untitled | 2007
17.8 CM IN DIAMETER
18-karat gold, 22-karat gold, 24-karat
gold, mandarin garnets, sapphires, rubies,
PHOTO BY R. H. HENSLEIGH

Ghazaleh Rabiei

The Flow of Charity | 2008

23 X 13 X 16 CM

Sterling silver, Persian turquoise; hand forged

PHOTO BY SARA S. MANESH

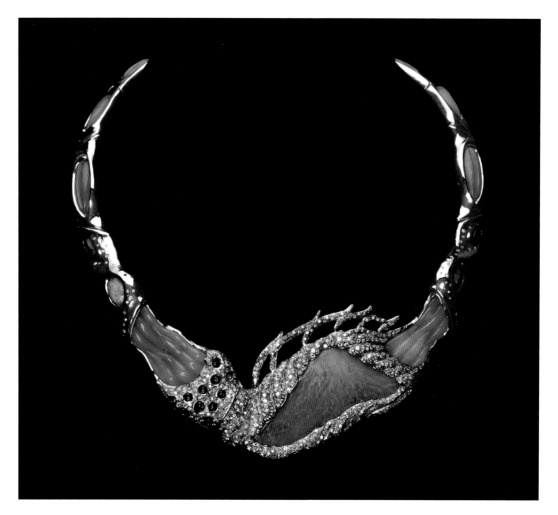

Daniel C. Toledo

Birth of an Opal Necklace | 2005

16.5 X 19 CM

18-karat white gold, black opal, diamonds, tanzanite,
Peruvian blue opal, chalcedony, chrysocolla

PHOTO BY ARTIST

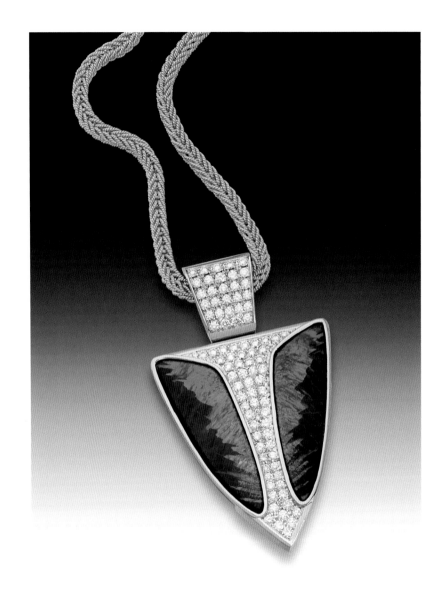

Barbara Westwood

Butterfly Opal | 2008

6 X 3.7 X 1 CM

Australian opal, 18-karat yellow gold, diamonds

PHOTO BY SKY HALL

Diana Vincent

Continuum Collection: Band | 2002

WIDTH, 1.6 CM

Platinum, diamonds

PHOTO BY WILLIAM HOOPER, COURTESY OF DE BEERS

Susan Helmich

Untitled | 2004

3.2 X 3 CM

Morganite, diamonds, 18-karat gold; cast

MORGANITE CUT BY TOM MUNSTEINER
PHOTO BY JOSH HELMICH

German Kabirski
Ring: Fire | 2008
2.3 X 2.7 X 3 CM
14-karat gold, white and black
diamonds, African black tree
PHOTO BY ARTIST

Paul Leathers
Untitled | 1986
2.4 X 2 X 1.8 CM
Sterling silver, rhodolite
garnets; cast, constructed
PHOTO BY ARTIST

Elena Kriegner
Sail Away | 2007
3 X 2.7 X 1.4 CM
18-karat white gold, aquamarine
PHOTO BY MARK KOCH

Michael Zobel

Brooch/Pendant | 2008

6.5 X 7 X 1.5 CM

18-karat rose gold, platinum,
aquamarine, raw diamond; fused

PHOTO BY FRED THOMAS

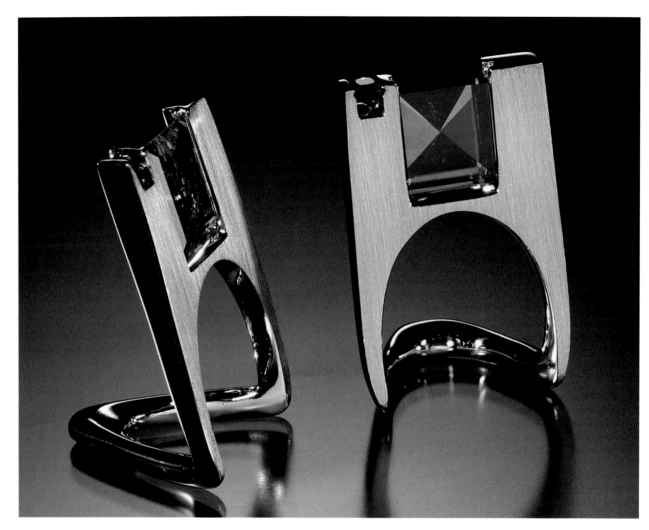

John Strobel

Stand Up Rings | 2007

1.8 X 2.5 X 3.3 CM

14-karat gold, tourmalines, princess-
cut sapphires; mirror cut, cast

PHOTO BY LARRY SANDERS

Chris Kuhta

Everyone Will Know You're Engaged to Me | 2006

3 X 1.8 X 1.3 CM

Diamond, sterling silver, 18-karat
gold; forged, fabricated, tension set

PHOTO BY ARTIST

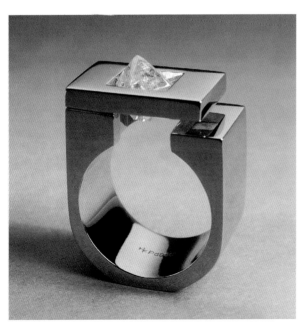

Niki Kavakonis

Tip of the Iceberg—Ring | 2007

3 X 2.2 X 1.2 CM

Canadian octahedral diamond, palladium

PHOTO BY ARTIST

Yael Herman

Sliding Diamonds—Rings | 2005

LEFT, 3.5 X 2.4 X 2.4 CM; RIGHT, 2.8 X 2.8 X 0.6 CM

Stainless steel, diamonds

PHOTO BY NATAN DVIR

Tom Munsteiner

Ring: Scissors | 2008

2.5 X 2 X 1.2 CM

Aquamarine, platinum

PHOTO BY ARTIST

Elena Kriegner

Überring | 2008

2.8 X 2.1 X 0.9 CM

18-karat white gold, lime citrine, topaz, citrine, amethyst, diamonds

PHOTO BY MARK KOCH

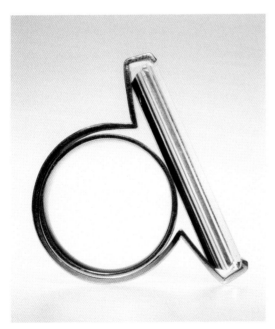

Mana Kehr

Topaz Stangen Ring | 2008

3 X 5 X 0.9 CM

Topaz, 18-karat white gold; hand fabricated

PHOTO BY JOSEF FISCHER

Mary Ann Buis

The Ice Box | 2007

4 X 1.7 X 0.7 CM

19-karat white gold, natural semi-cut aquamarine crystal, round brilliant-cut diamonds; handcrafted, channel set, pavé set

PHOTO BY CARLA WILSON

Eleanor Moty

Glacial Brooch | 2008

5.2 X 5.4 X 1.4 CM

Sterling silver, 18-karat gold, quartz, stem pearl

PHOTO BY ARTIST

Geoffrey D. Giles

Untitled | 2008

4.5 X 1.5 X 0.8 CM

18-karat palladium white gold, tourmalated quartz, diamonds; hand fabricated, bezel set, flush set, hand engraved

PHOTO BY ARTIST

So Maruyama

Notch Grip | 2007

2.4 X 2 X 0.6 CM

Diamond, titanium; filed

PHOTO BY ARTIST

The Cleo Collection
Promise Forever Series: Captured | 2006
2.7 X 2.3 X 0.6 CM
18-karat white gold, 18-karat pink gold, diamonds; cast
PHOTOS BY RAFFIX

Patricia Tschetter

Bumper Cars | 2005

3.8 X 2.4 X 2.4 CM

Trillion-cut tanzanite, trillion-cut spessartite garnet, trillion-cut Paraiba tourmaline, white round diamonds, 18-karat white palladium, 22-karat yellow gold; fabricated, granulated, riveted, hollow constructed

PHOTO BY ROBERT DIAMANTE

Chris Ploof

Holey Stuffed Bangle | 2007

DIAMETER, 7.5 CM

Sterling silver, cubic zirconia

PHOTO BY HAP SAKWA

Karl Fritsch

Licht Durch Fall | 2007

3.8 X 2 X 1 CM

Gold, rubellite

PHOTO BY ARTIST

Sara Blaine
Aegean Scroll Collection | 2008
Sterling silver, 22-karat gold, semiprecious gemstones
PHOTO BY JAIME MAYNARD

Nina Basharova
Rock Candy Rings | 2006
3 X 2.2 X 1.5 CM
18-karat gold, diamonds, tourmaline, peridot
PHOTO BY NAOYA FUJISHIRO

Dauvit Alexander, the Justified Sinner
Three Post-Apocalyptic Cocktail Rings | 2008
ROUND, 6.5 X 3 X 2.5 CM; THREADED, 4 X 3.5 X 3.5 CM; SQUARE, 4.7 X 3.5 X 3.5 CM

Iron, silver, peridot, blue topaz, tourmaline, lemon citrine,
garnets, green cubic zirconia, pale citrine, amethyst; set

PHOTO BY ANDREW NEILSON, NEILSON PHOTOGRAPHY

Shay Lahover

Untitled | 2007

2.5 X 1.9 X 1.9 CM

18-karat gold, 24-karat gold, uncut
ruby, drusy, rubies, diamonds

PHOTO BY R. H. HENSLEIGH

Keeyoon Kang

Cake Ring | 2001

2.5 X 1.3 X 3.8 CM

22-karat gold, sapphire, champagne
diamonds, silver; granulated

PHOTOS BY STUDIO MUNCH

So Simple! Would work with shell shapes.

Robin Rotenier

Rotenier Pétale Necklace | 2008

44.5 X 1.9 X 0.7 CM

Sterling silver, 18-karat gold, diamonds; hand carved

PHOTO BY ARTIST

Jurio Fujita

Mask Ring | 2007

2.8 X 2 X 3.5 CM

18-karat yellow gold, diamonds, alexandrites; lost wax cast

PHOTO BY ARTIST

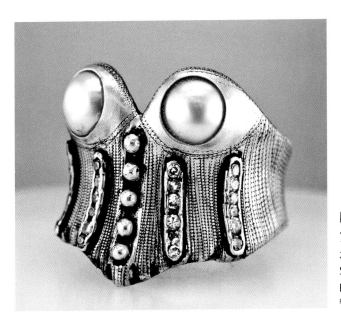

Michelle A. Lanier

The Grand Duchess Corset Ring | 2008

2.1 X 2.3 X 2.5 CM

Sterling silver, fine silver, cultured silver rose pearls, diamonds; mock channel set

PHOTO BY ARTIST

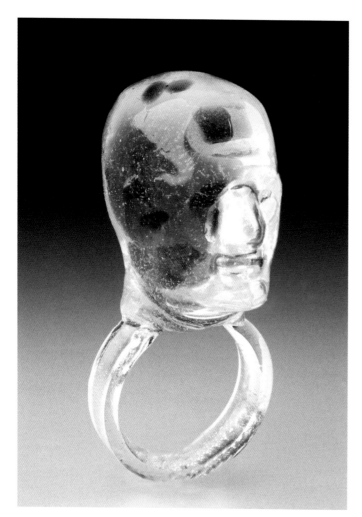

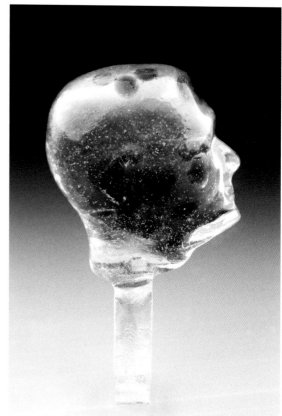

Stevie B.

Headstone | 2008

5.5 X 2.6 X 3.1 CM

Epoxy resin, amethyst, Burma ruby, iolite, London
Blue topaz, peridot, rhodolite garnet, watermelon
tourmaline; cast, filed, sanded, polished

PHOTOS BY ARTIST

Settling for opal?

Zamama Metal Arts Studio
I Love Taiwan | 2008
6 X 3.5 X 0.6 CM
Sterling silver, jade
PHOTO BY ARTIST

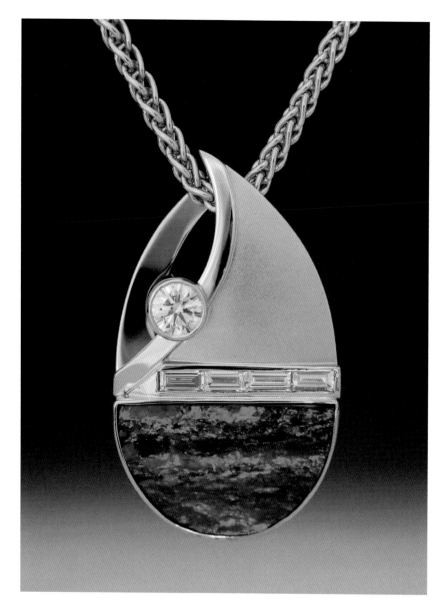

Patrick Murphy

Untitled | 2006

4 X 2.5 X 1 CM

14-karat gold, opal doublet, diamonds

PHOTO BY COREY MORSE

Sonja Picard
Naga Kanya Ring | 2008
4 X 3 X 2 CM
14-karat yellow gold, checkerboard blue topaz, diamonds
PHOTO BY TYLER GARNHAM

Elizabeth Ann Tokoly
Trapeze Artist | 2008
3.4 X 3 X 0.6 CM; CHAIN, 40.6 CM LONG
18-karat gold, diamond; forged
PHOTO BY D. JAMES DEE

Karen Bizer

Mandala | 2008

2 X 2 X 1.8 CM

Star ruby, 18-karat yellow gold, white diamonds;
hand carved, prong set, hand engraved, pavé set

PHOTO BY D. JAMES DEE

Chao-Hsien Kuo

Ice Flower | 2005

4 X 2.5 X 2 CM

Rock crystal, 18-karat yellow gold; goldsmithed

PHOTOS BY ARTIST

L. Sue Szabo

Bauble | 2007

3.2 X 4.7 X 4.7 CM

14-karat gold, 18-karat gold, faceted rubies, colored sapphires,
vintage watch crystal; hand fabricated, bezel set

PHOTO BY ERICA CRISSMAN, WIRED IMAGES

Jen Townsend

Dragon Temple | 2008

6 X 5 X 0.6 CM

18-karat gold, silver, boulder opal, sapphire; fabricated

PHOTO BY ARTIST

Susan Foster

Tree of Life Ring | 2008

2.6 X 0.2 CM

22-karat yellow gold, Peruvian opal;
hand crafted, hand hammered

PHOTO BY ARTIST

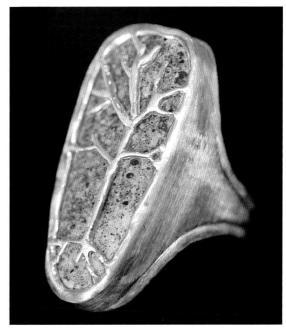

Natasha Wozniak

Citrine Navette Ring | 2007

4.7 X 3.5 X 3.3 CM

22-karat gold, sterling silver, citrine, tourmaline;
fabricated, fused, forged, tapered

PHOTO BY ARTIST

could be adapted into water – bubbles, with fish

Belle Brooke Barer

Moonrise Necklace | 2008

42 CM LONG

Sterling silver, 18-karat gold, champagne
diamonds; oxidized, hand fabricated, cast, soldered

PHOTO BY GEORGE POST

Davide Bigazzi

Vinci Cuff | 2008

3.8 X 6.6 X 5.6 CM

Sterling silver, 18-karat gold, black
diamonds; hand forged, hand fabricated

PHOTO BY HAP SAKWA

Keith Lewis

Mica and Ruby Brooch | 2007

4 X 4 X 0.5 CM

Mica sheets, pearls, ruby cabochon,
23-karat gold leaf; layered, shellacked

PHOTO BY RALPH GABRINER

Wesley Glebe

Jacquie's Ring | 2008

0.6 X 2.3 X 0.2 CM

Titanium, peridot, 14-karat yellow
gold, 24-karat gold; cold connected

PHOTO BY PAUL JEREMIAS

Meredith Robb

Captured Ruby Necklace | 2008

20 X 15 X 1 CM

Stainless-steel washers, ruby ball bearings, 18-karat gold

PHOTO BY PAUL AMBTMAN

Julie Mikelson
Jade and Brass Ring | 2006
11.4 X 3.8 X 2.5 CM
Brass, sterling silver, jade
PHOTO BY BECKY MCDONAH

Cynthia Gorman
Diamond Barnacles | 2006
4 X 4 X 0.5 CM
Palladium, 14-karat rose gold,
round diamonds; hand fabricated
PHOTO BY RICK RAPHAEL

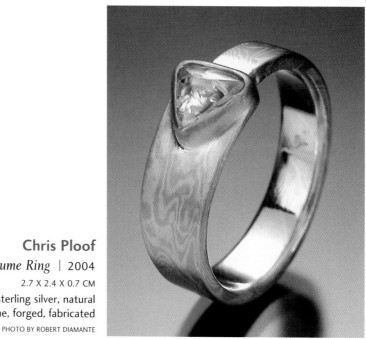

Chris Ploof
Natural Diamond Mokume Ring | 2004
2.7 X 2.4 X 0.7 CM
18-karat yellow gold, sterling silver, natural
diamond; mokume gane, forged, fabricated
PHOTO BY ROBERT DIAMANTE

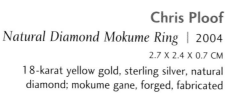

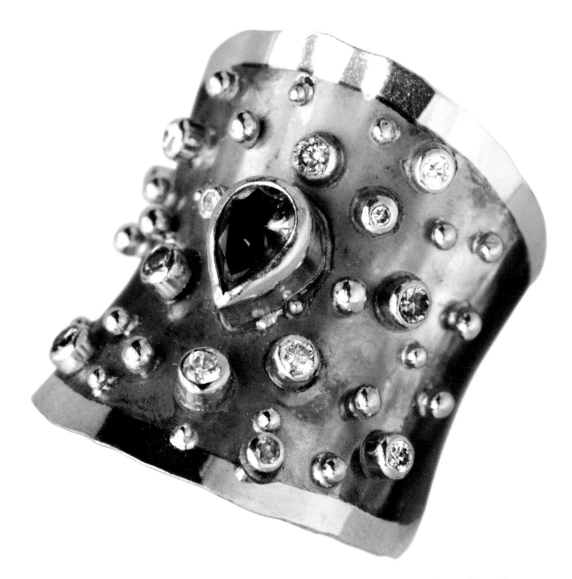

Josephine Bergsøe
Starry Night | 2007
3.5 X .2 CM
22-karat gold, silver, diamonds; oxidized, soldered, forged
PHOTO BY SARA LINDBAEK

Haya Elfasi and Efrat Nordman
Mumtaz—Indian Diamond Ring | 2007
3 X 3 X 2.3 CM
18-karat gold, rough green diamonds, rose-cut diamond, green tourmaline
PHOTO BY YARON WEINBERG

Shay Lahover
Green Sun | 2007
7.5 X 7.5 CM
18-karat gold, 24-karat gold,
tourmaline, diamonds; handmade
PHOTO BY YOSSI ZWECKER

Keeyoon Kang
Untitled | 2005
EACH, 1.9 X 1.9 CM
22-karat gold, peridot
PHOTO BY STUDIO MUNCH

Kadri Mälk

Invisible Hands | 2001

24 X 9.5 X 0.4 CM

Silver, almandines, Cibatool, jade, coral,
rhodolite, black pearls, beads; engraved, cut

PHOTO BY TANEL VEENRE

Anna Ruth Henriques

To Be or Not To Be | 2008

5.5 X 5 X 1.4 CM

18-karat gold, rock crystal, moonstone,
mother-of-pearl, white diamond, original painting

PHOTO BY GAETANO SALVADORE

Gunilla Lantz

The Nest | 2008

5.5 CM IN DIAMETER

Silver, 18-karat gold, spider grey
moonstone, diamonds; oxidized

PHOTO BY HANS BJURLING

Sonya Ooten

Untitled | 2008

EACH, 4.5 X 3 CM

18-karat gold, white diamonds, champagne diamonds

PHOTO BY SEAN BURNS

Ulla Ahola

Brooch | 2008

15 X 7 X 1.4 CM

Jasper, hematite, synthetic ruby,
silver, cotton thread; handmade

PHOTO BY JUHO AHOLA

Charles Lewton-Brain

Dappled Pendant, Cage Series B674 | 2008

5 X 4.5 X 2 CM

Stainless steel, copper, 24-karat gold, agate,
moonstone, rubies; electroformed

PHOTO BY ARTIST

Jennifer Hall

Untitled Brooch | 2008

7.6 X 4.4 X 2.5 CM

Copper, steel, silver, paper, paint, colored pencil, graphite
pencil, epoxy resin, tourmaline; hand fabricated

PHOTO BY DOUG YAPLE

Diane Weimer

Seascape | 2008

6.5 X 6.4 X 1 CM

Argentium silver, sterling silver, stone,
Willow Creek jasper cabochon; overlaid

PHOTO BY ARTIST

Federica Rettore

Cuff | 2008

16 CM IN DIAMETER

Gold, steel, diamonds, tourmaline
quartz, zebu horn

PHOTO BY ARTIST

Andréia Sutter
Roberto Sutter

Swiss Alps Ring | 2007

3.3 X 3.9 X 3 CM

Black slate with pyrite inclusions from the Swiss Alps,
diamonds, 18-karat yellow gold; cut, polished

PHOTO BY ROBERTO SUTTER

Dauvit Alexander, the Justified Sinner

Blue Sunset on the Grey Lagoon | 2008

30 X 20 X 3 CM

Iron, silver, discarded sewing machine needles, discarded dental
burr, steel, porcelain, freshwater pearls, aventurine, aquamarine,
peridot, amethyst, nephrite, blue topaz, tsavorite garnet

PHOTO BY ANDREW NEILSON, NEILSON PHOTOGRAPHY

Eily O'Connell
Clutch | 2008
11 X 3 X 2 CM
Silver, rough-cut aquamarine; cast, oxidized
PHOTO BY NORTON ASSOCIATES

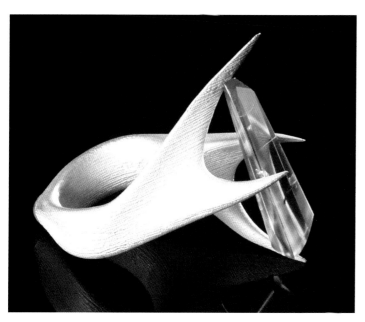

Hagen Gamisch
Aedes Sapientia | 2006
5 X 4.6 X 3 CM
Silver, aquamarine; CAD, sandcast, cut
PHOTO BY PETRA JASCHKE

Nina Basharova

Song of the Stars: Nightingale's Nest | 2007

6.5 X 6.5 X 2 CM

18-karat gold, diamonds, Tahitian pearls, feathers

PHOTO BY NAOYA FUJISHIRO

Jee Hye Kwon

Eternity | 2008

3.8 X 2.5 X 3 CM

24-karat gold, 18-karat gold, silver, quartz;
hand fabricated, textured, kum boo, prong set

PHOTO BY RALPH GABRINER

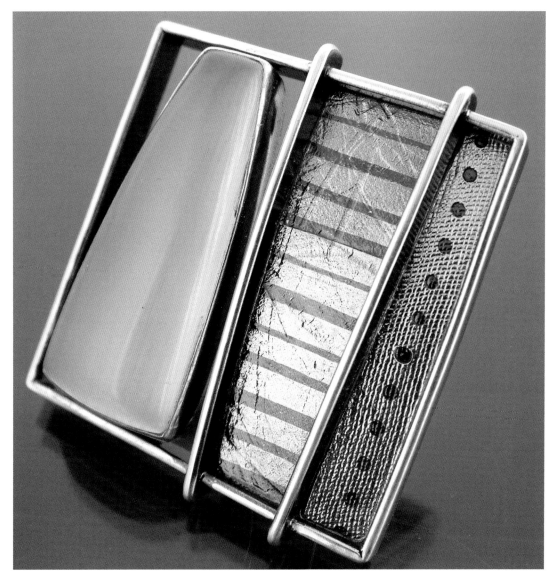

Birgit Kupke-Peyla
Square Exploration #3 | 2008
4.3 X 4.3 X 1 CM
Sterling silver, 22-karat gold, palladium,
aquamarine; fused, carved, fabricated
PHOTO BY ARTIST

Regine Schwarzer

Brooches | 2007

LEFT, 5.6 X 3.6 X 0.8 CM; RIGHT, 3.7 X 5.4 X 0.8 CM

Jasperoid, chrysoprase, sterling silver, 24-karat gold; hand cut

PHOTO BY STEVE WILSON

Marina Elenskaya

Untitled | 2008

4 X 5.5 X 6.5 CM

Wood, chrysophase

PHOTO BY FEDERICO CAVICCHIOLI

Kristina Glick Shank

Memory's Pieces: Islands | 2006

45 X 7 X 2 CM

Stones, coral fragments, sea glass, snail shells, sterling silver

PHOTO BY ARTIST

Beth Humphrey, RW Wise Goldsmiths Inc.

18K Lacy Dendritic Agate Pendant | 2008

3.8 X 3.8 X 0.9 CM

18-karat gold, dendritic agate; hand pierced

PHOTO BY ARTIST

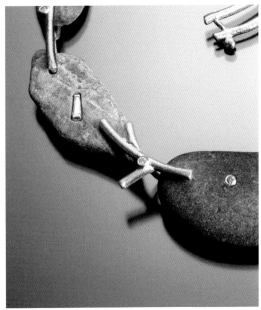

Patricia Daunis-Dunning
Rocks and Stones | 2006
51 CM LONG
18-karat gold, white diamonds, champagne
diamonds, stones; drilled, carved, set, riveted
PHOTOS BY ROBERT DIAMANTE

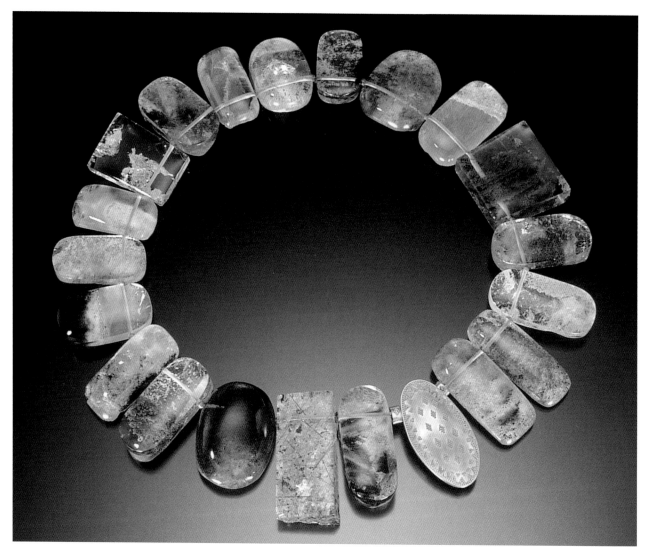

Jill Hurant

Untitled | 2003

3.8 X 43.2 CM

22-karat gold, dendritic quartz; hand fabricated, granulated

PHOTO BY RALPH GABRINER

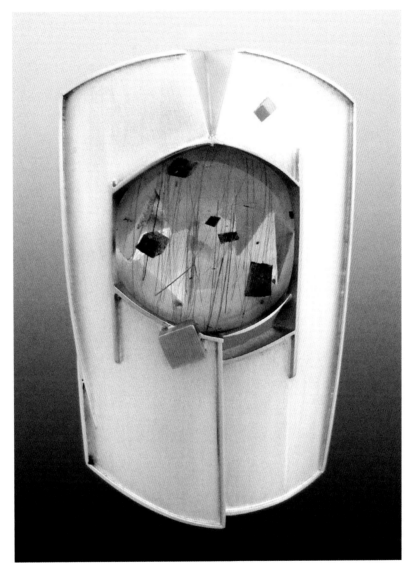

Eleanor Moty

Celestial Brooch | 2007

7 X 4.5 X 1.5 CM

Sterling silver, 22-karat gold, rutilated
quartz with mineral inclusions

QUARTZ BY TOM MUNSTEINER
PHOTO BY ARTIST

Valerie Jo Coulson

Skylights Cuff | 2006

7 X 8 X 0.8 CM

Sterling silver, tourmalated quartz; fabricated, bezel set

PHOTO BY CURTIS HALDY

Hirose Chibimaru Tomonori
Intellectual Offering | 2007
2.6 X 2.4 X 0.6 CM
Zirconium, diamond, tantalum; machine cut, anodized, cold forged

Simone Giesen

Untitled | 2008

3.6 X 6.7 X 1.2 CM

Sterling silver, lace, prasiolite, stainless steel; hand fabricated

PHOTO BY ARTIST

Ingeborg Vandamme
Reflection | 2008

7 X 7.5 X 2 CM

Rock crystal, aluminium, brass, waxed
cord, rubber, thread; anodized, painted

PHOTO BY ARTIST

Yeonkyung Kim
Variation III (Brooch) | 2004

5.4 X 4.6 X 2.6 CM

Smoky quartz with rutile, 18-karat gold-plated
sterling silver, stainless steel; cut, fabricated

PHOTO BY KWANG-CHUN PARK (KC STUDIO)

Beppe Kessler
Mother and Son | 2005
DIAMETER, 25 CM
Gold, opal, jet
PHOTO BY TOM HAARTSEN

Yeonkyung Kim
Variation I (Brooch) | 2004
13 X 6 X 1.4 CM
Amethyst, smoky quartz, platinum-plated
sterling silver, stainless steel; cut, fabricated
PHOTO BY KWANG-CHUN PARK (KC STUDIO)

Dieter Lorenz
Carved Citrine Pendant | 2007
1.9 X 3.1 X 1.9 CM
Citrine, elephant hair; carved
PHOTO BY LICHTBLICK PHOTODESIGN

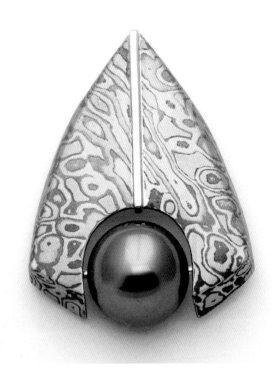

James Binnion
Pendant | 2007
3.5 X 2.7 X 1.2 CM
18-karat yellow gold, iron, Tahitian pearl; mokume gane
PHOTO BY ARTIST

Gintare Kizys
Untitled | 2008
LEFT, 1 X 1.2 X 0.8 CM; RIGHT, 1.2 X 2.1 X 1.3 CM
Phantom quartz, 18-karat rose gold,
diamonds, European shank; brushed finish
PHOTO BY ARTIST

Christine Hafermalz-Wheeler

Cocktail Ring | 2008

4.5 X 2 X 3 CM

Tourmaline quartz, Cook Island
black pearl, 18-karat yellow gold

TOURMALINE QUARTZ BY TOM MUNSTEINER
PHOTOS BY DAVID WHEELER

Christoph Freier

Doublerings | 2008

EACH, 5 CM WIDE

18-karat gold, green tourmalines, sterling silver, garnets

PHOTO BY ARTIST

Gillian Hillerud

Paper Brooch | 2008

6.4 X 7.6 X 1 CM

Silver, 14-karat gold, paper, pearls, blue topaz, cubic zirconia, moonstone, thread; hand fabricated

PHOTO BY VICKY LAM

Hui-Mei Pan

Three | 2007

4.6 X 4 X 1.9 CM

Sterling silver, amethyst, pebble; oxidized, bezel set, prong set

PHOTO BY ARTIST

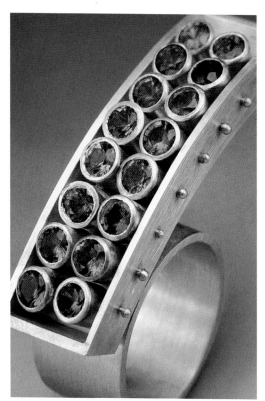

L. Sue Szabo

Sway (kinetic) | 2007

2.8 X 1 X 4 CM

Sterling silver, pink sapphires, Burmese ruby; hand fabricated, tube set

PHOTO BY ERICA CRISSMAN, WIRED IMAGES

Sofia Tenthio

Rainbow Ring | 2007

1.3 CM IN DIAMETER

18-karat white gold, 18-karat yellow gold, pink tourmaline, blue sapphires

PHOTO BY ARTIST

Ivan Sagel

Eye of Horus | 2006

3 X 2 X 1 CM

18-karat gold, stainless steel, sterling silver, round
white diamonds, pink tourmaline; tension set

PHOTO BY GUY NICOL

Yael Sonia

Perpetual Motion: Spinning Wheel | 2000

8.3 CM IN DIAMETER

18-karat yellow gold, blue topaz, diamonds; hand constructed

PHOTO BY ALMIR PASTORE

Tom Munsteiner
Necklace: Scissors | 2008
4.6 X 6.1 X 1.6 CM
Paraiba tourmaline, 18-karat yellow gold, black jade
PHOTO BY ARTIST

Erica Courtney

18K Gold and Diamond Goddess Rings | 2005

VARIOUS DIMENSIONS

Yellow beryl, green beryl, peridot, kunzite, topaz, 18-karat gold, diamonds

PHOTO BY JAY GOLDMAN

Paula Crevoshay

Ocean Dream | 2005

8.3 X 5.1 X 1.6 CM

18-karat gold, chrysocolla, moonstone, diamonds,
zircon; carved, hand fabricated, layered, bead set,
prong set, bezel set, pierced, engraved, granulated

CARVED BY GLENN LEHRER
PHOTOS BY PETER HURST

377

ZIL

Blue Sea Pendant | 2007

2.5 X 2 X 0.6 CM

Blue topaz, tsavorite garnets, 18-karat gold

PHOTO BY EDUARDO CONTE

Nicole Landaw

Amethyst Long Water Droplet Earrings | 2008

EACH, 4.4 X 1.3 X 1.3 CM

18-karat gold, Brazilian amethysts; cut, cast, set, finished

PHOTO BY RSP MEDIA

Paula Crevoshay
Kunzite Orchid Rings | 2008
EACH, 3.2 X 2.5 X 3.5 CM
Kunzite, sapphire, amethyst, diamonds, Iolite
PHOTO BY PETER HURST

Kent Raible

Moonflower Ring | 2008

3.5 X 3.5 X 2.5 CM

18-karat gold, rainbow moonstone, garnets,
diamonds; fabricated, granulated, bezel set

PHOTO BY HAP SAKWA

380

Lilly Fitzgerald
Moonstone Pendant | 2008

4.5 X 2 X 1.5 CM

White moonstone, 22-karat gold; hand fabricated

PHOTO BY HAP SAKWA

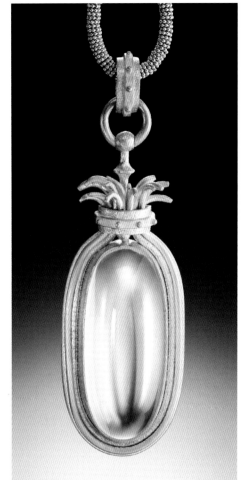

Kristin Hanson Jewelry
Diamond Ring | 2006

3.1 X 1.5 X 0.4 CM

18-karat yellow gold, diamonds

PHOTO BY ANTHONY M. PUOPOLO

Jack Gualtieri, Zaffiro Jewelry
Patricia Pendant | 2008

4.5 X 2 X 1.2 CM

Mint green beryl, diamonds, 22-karat yellow gold,
18-karat yellow gold; set, fused, granulated

PHOTO BY DANIEL VAN ROSSEN

**Julie Lynn Romanenko
for Just Jules, LLC**

It's All About the Blues | 2007

2 X 2 X 1 CM

14-karat gold, natural rough-cut Brazilian
aquamarine, round diamond; wax carved

PHOTO BY RAM PHOTOGRAPHY

Kent Raible

Untitled | 2008

EACH, 6 X 2.5 X 1.5 CM

18-karat gold, rainbow moonstones, pink sapphires,
tanzanites, aquamarines; fabricated, granulated, bezel set

PHOTO BY HAP SAKWA

Greg Christian

Kite Wing | 2008

3 X 1.9 X 0.8 CM

Peridot, 14-karat white gold, 14-karat
yellow gold, white diamonds

PHOTO BY CHRIS ADYNIEC

Julia Behrends
Lock Love Engagement Ring | 2003
3 X 2.2 X 1.6 CM
Platinum, diamond, melee diamond accents
PHOTO BY ROBERT DIAMANTE

Sara D. Commers

Majestic Spessartite | 2007

3 X 3 X 1 CM

14-karat yellow gold, spessartite garnet, round brilliant diamonds

GEMSTONE FACETED BY TATYANA VYALKIN
PHOTO BY ROBERT CAMPBELL

Katy Briscoe

18K YG Cognac Tourmaline and Diamond Ring in Columns Mounting | 2008

TOURMALINE, 1.6 X 2 CM

18-karat yellow gold, oval tourmaline, trillion-cut tourmalines, diamonds; bezel set

PHOTOS BY KENNON EVETT

Nicole Landaw

Rutilated Quartz Teardrop Pendant | 2008

PENDANT, 4.8 X 2.5 X 1.3 CM

18-karat gold, rutilated quartz; cut, cast, set, finished

PHOTO BY RSP MEDIA

George Sawyer

Untitled | 1998

20 X 20 X 2 CM

Pink topaz, 18-karat yellow gold, platinum,
14-karat red gold, diamonds, sapphires;
mokume gane, hand fabricated

PHOTO BY ARTIST

Stephanie Albertson

Mosaic Cuff | 2008

5.1 CM WIDE

22-karat gold, rose-cut sapphire,
aquamarine, tourmaline, peridot;
handcrafted

PHOTO BY DAVID LEWIS TAYLOR

Karin Worden

Flower with Aqua Leaf | 2008

7.6 X 5.7 X 1.3 CM

Sterling silver, 22-karat gold, 24-karat gold, 18-karat palladium white gold, yellow sapphires, aquamarine, rhodolite garnet; fabricated, fused, embossed

PHOTO BY HAP SAKWA

Conni Mainne

Isis' Dream | 2007

4.5 X 4 X 1.5 CM

18-karat yellow gold,
aquamarine, diamonds,
South Sea pearl; cast, fabricated

PHOTO BY RALPH GABRINER

Diana Vincent

Kaiyu-Shiki Earrings | 2006

EACH, 3.2 X 2.5 X 0.3 CM

18-karat yellow gold, marquise-
shaped serpentine stone, labradorite,
Mexican opal; handmade

PHOTO BY DIANA VINCENT INC.

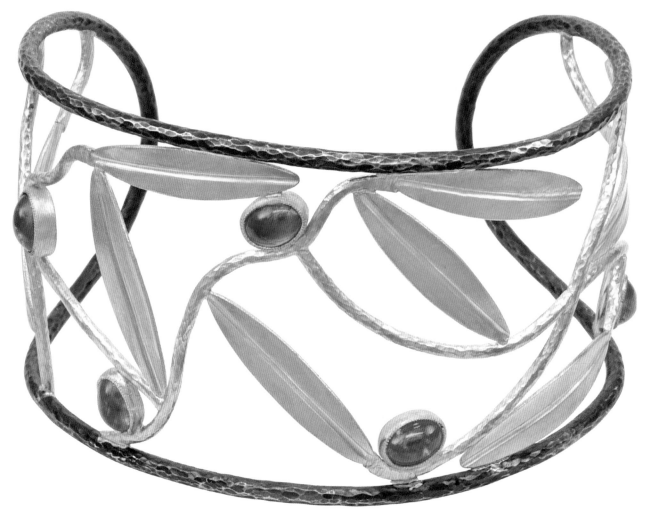

Lika Behar

24K Olive Branch Cuff | 2008

15 CM IN DIAMETER

24-karat gold, silver, cabochon emeralds; hand fabricated, oxidized

PHOTO BY ARTIST

Natasha Wozniak

Hanging Fronds Earrings | 2007

EACH, 6 X 2 X 0.5 CM

18-karat gold, 22-karat gold, sterling silver,
tourmaline; chased, repoussé, forged, soldered

PHOTO BY ARTIST

Danielle Meshorer

Remnants of the Wedding Bouquet | 2008

2.5 X 5.1 X 3 CM

18-karat yellow gold, Mexican fire opals, sapphires,
jade marquis; CAD designed, cast, bent

PHOTO BY HAP SAKWA

Daphne Krinos
Necklace | 2007
4 X 0.5 CM; 48 CM LONG
Silver, beryls, citrines; oxidized
PHOTO BY PETER WHITE, FXP

Jee Hye Kwon

Boundaries | 2008

7.1 X 5.1 X 6.4 CM

Silver, pearls, diamonds; hand fabricated, prong set

PHOTO BY RALPH GABRINER

Keith Lewis

Mica Brooch | 2008

3.7 X 5 X .5 CM

Mica, ruby, black pearl, 23-karat gold leaf; layered, shellacked

PHOTO BY RALPH GABRINER

Todd A. Pownell

Mountain Trail Sunset | 2007

LARGE SQUARE, 3.5 X 3.7 X 1 CM; SMALL SQUARE, 1.7 X 2 X 1 CM

Sterling silver, round diamonds, 24-karat yellow gold, red
gemstones, natural round rubies, garnets; hand fabricated

PHOTO BY DAN FOX, LUMINA STUDIOS

Jennifer Kellogg
Sparkle Earrings | 1994
EACH, 2.5 X 2.3 X 0.7 CM
18-karat gold, amethyst
PHOTO BY LUIS ERNESTO SANTANA

Diana Weiss Widman
Montana Sapphire Cascade | 2008
7.6 X 5.8 X 0.6 CM
Montana sapphire crystal, violet spinel,
18-karat gold; fold formed, fabricated
PHOTO BY STEVE WAGNER

Babette Von Dohnanyi
Untitled | 2007
EACH, 3 X 2.5 X 2 CM
Sterling silver, amethyst, rose crystal; cut, cast
PHOTO BY FEDERICO CAVICCHIOLI

James Kaya
Total Eclipse | 2006
2.5 X 1.9 CM
Pearl, sapphire, diamonds; hand fabricated
PHOTO BY ROBERT DIAMANTE

Boline Strand

Cupolae Necklace | 2007

1.7 X 5.1 X 44 CM

White diamonds, seed pearls, 22-karat gold, 18-karat gold, sterling silver; hand fabricated, beaded, bezel set

PHOTO BY TOM MILLS

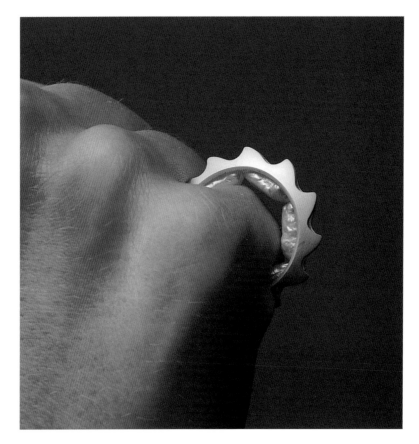

Miriam Verbeek

Cog-Wheel-Ring | 1993

2.8 CM IN DIAMETER

Silver, pearls

PHOTO BY H. VAN BEEK

Sasha Samuels

Two-Pearl Ring | 2002

2.8 X 2.3 X 1.2 CM

18-karat white gold, South Sea faceted
pearls, natural colored diamonds

PHOTO BY DANIEL VAN ROSSEN

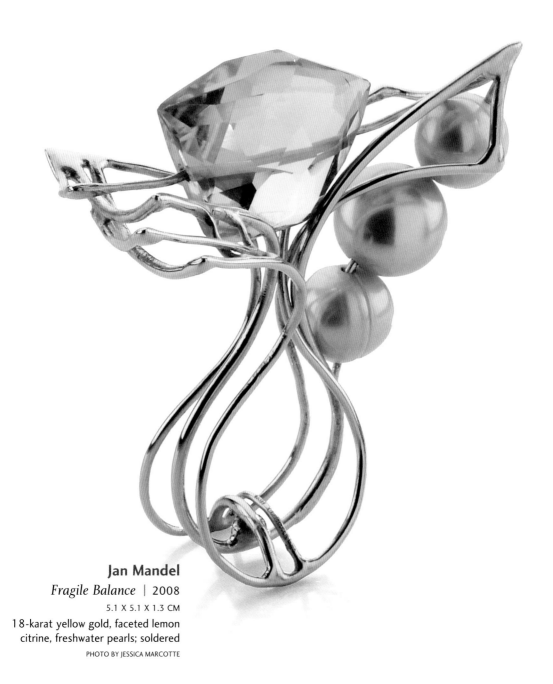

Jan Mandel

Fragile Balance | 2008

5.1 X 5.1 X 1.3 CM

18-karat yellow gold, faceted lemon
citrine, freshwater pearls; soldered

PHOTO BY JESSICA MARCOTTE

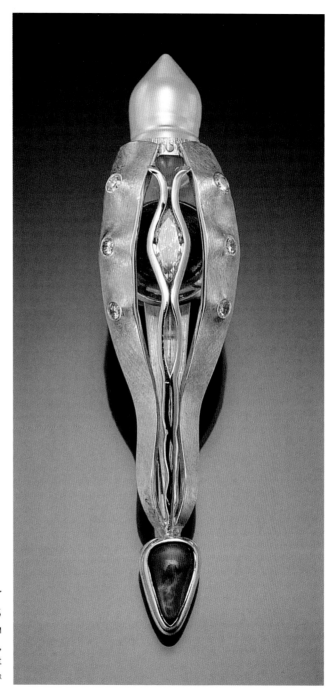

Wayne Werner

Artemis Brooch | 2006

5 X 2 X 2 CM

18-karat gold, platinum, opal, pearl,
diamonds, ruby; forged, set

PHOTO BY RALPH GABRINER

Lisa Cylinder
Scott Cylinder

Old Ball Gamebird Brooch | 1999

7 X 9 X 2 CM

Sterling silver, brass, ash, 18-karat bimetal, cubic zirconia, leather
baseball cover, flocking, patina; fabricated, formed, carved

PHOTO BY JEFFREY K. BRADY

Stephan Hoglund
Lady of the Lake | 2007
7 X 7 CM
18-karat gold, thomsonite, black drusy onyx
PHOTO BY ARTIST

Linda Kindler Priest

Lion Walk Brooch | 2000

4 X 6.3 X 0.4 CM

14-karat gold, diamonds; repoussé

PHOTO BY GORDON BERNSTEIN

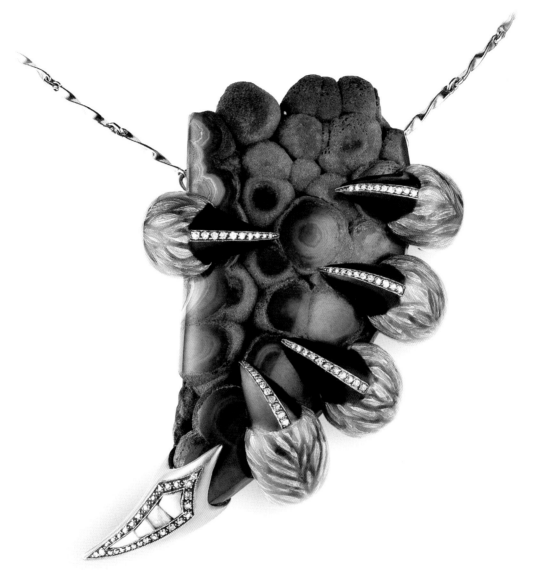

Pandora Barthen

The Klaw | 2007

9.6 X 5.8 CM

18-karat yellow gold, enamel, rose-cut
diamond, opal, malachite drusy; inlaid

PHOTO BY LEE WOOLDRIDGE

Peter Schmid, Atelier Zobel

Brooch/Pendant | 2008

3.5 X 14 X 6 CM

Sterling silver, 22-karat gold, 24-karat gold, tourmaline; welded, lasered

PHOTO BY FRED THOMAS

Michael Manthey

Harmony | 2005

5.1 X 7 X 1.9 CM

Pyrope garnet, green garnets, rainbow moonstone, carved slate,
opals, citrine, sterling silver, fine silver, 14-karat-gold, 18-karat gold

PHOTO BY ARTIST

Jennifer Kellogg

Pavé Diamond Outline Pendant | 2004

PENDANT, 1.5 X 2 X 0.3 CM; CHAIN, 40 CM LONG

14-karat white gold, diamonds

PHOTO BY LUIS ERNESTO SANTANA

Jennifer Rabe Morin

Rock Star | 2008

3.7 X 3 X 3 CM

18-karat white gold, pink sapphire, diamonds,
star rose quartz cabochon; cast, pavé set

PHOTO BY GREGORY MORIN

Diana Vincent

Continuum Collection: Ring | 2002

WIDTH, 1.5 CM

Platinum, diamonds

PHOTO BY WILLIAM HOOPER, COURTESY OF DE BEERS

Gumuchian

Bahia Earrings | 2008

EACH, 5.5 X 1.5 X 0.2 CM

Round brilliant diamonds, pink sapphire, amethysts, rubies

PHOTO BY KAREN JANOWSKI

Jeffrey E. Appling
American Ingenuity | 2003–2007

24 X 18 CM

Ametrine, chrome tourmaline, 14-karat white gold, drusy onyx, natural gemstones; hand fabricated, cast, carved, drilled

PHOTOS BY HAP SAKWA

Gillian E. Batcher
Untitled | 2008
PENDANT, 3.6 X 3 X 0.6 CM
14-karat palladium white gold, sphene,
tsavorite garnets, sapphires; cast, fabricated
PHOTO BY PAUL AMBTMAN

Contributing Artists

Acknowledgments

I couldn't have imagined a more suitable colleague to jury this wonderful collection of jewelry than Cindy Edelstein. Her inquisitive spirit and thoughtful approach to the task at hand led to many great discussions about the science, nature, and sheer beauty of gems. Narrowing down all the beautiful images to 500 representatives in the field is no simple feat, but Cindy did it with skill, knowledge, and tireless enthusiasm. She has a sixth sense when it comes to recognizing top quality designs, and her appreciation for outstanding photography is a rare treat. Thank you, Cindy, for your passion and dedication.

The continued support of all the jewelers around the world who send images to be considered for this series never ceases to amaze me. This book is a celebration of their talent, creative vision, and dedication to their medium. I also wish to thank the galleries, schools, and organizations that promote contemporary jewelry, teach and inspire others, and advocate our publications.

I'm thankful for Lark Books' stellar team of professionals who manage the intense deadlines and numerous details that comprise these publications. Julie Hale, Dawn Dillingham, and Gavin Young provided superb editorial oversight and assistance. Chris Bryant, Kristi Pfeffer, Shannon Yokeley, and Bradley Norris supplied first-rate support in the art department, and designer Celia Naranjo produced a beautiful cover. Thanks to art director Matt Shay, who provided us with yet another gorgeous layout and design. Todd Kaderabek and Lance Wille made sure we were on schedule. Thank you all for making this book such a pleasure to create.

—Marthe Le Van

About the Juror

Cindy Edelstein began her career as a writer for *JCK* magazine, the nation's leading jewelry publication. She now heads the Jeweler's Resource Bureau, a business that supports the growth of jewelry design entrepreneurs. She is also involved with www.jewelersresource.com, which provides information and business coaching to jewelry designers, and www.JewelryDesignerFinder.com, a network of the best contemporary jewelers. She has written articles about the jewelry design business for many industry publications and consumer magazines.

Cindy has received high honors from the American Jewelry Design Council, the Contemporary Design Group, and the Women's Jewelry Association. She has presented hundreds of workshops and is deeply involved in Internet communications for jewelry. She maintains a blog, www.jewelrybusinessguru.typepad.com, where she shares tips and trends. Cindy also participates in Twitter (JewelryBizGuru) and Facebook. She lives in Pelham, New York.